# MAMA
# &
# THE HUNGRY HOLE

**NUMBER 4**

**WORDCRAFT SERIES OF FABULIST NOVELLAS**

# MAMA & the HUNGRY HOLE

## JOHANNA DeBIASE

La Grande, OR • 2015

# Acknowledgments

Copyright © 2015, Johanna DeBiase
ISBN: 978-1-877655-85-2
Library of Congress Control Number: 2015933291

Number Four in the Wordcraft Series of Fabulist Novellas

First Edition
June 1, 2015

Cover Design: Kristin Summers, www.redbatdesign.com
Cover graphics © DepositPhotos.com
Author photo: Judith DeBiase

Published by
Wordcraft of Oregon, LLC
PO Box 3235
La Grande, OR 97850
http://www.wordcraftoforegon.com
info@wordcraftoforegon.com

Member of Council of Literary Magazines & Presses (CLMP)

Text set in Garamond Premier Pro
Printed in United States

*For mothers everywhere
who smile despite it all
and for my daughter, Flora,
who keeps a smile on my face
despite it all*

"Dream is the personalized myth, myth the depersonalized dream; both myth and dream are symbolic in the same general way of the dynamic of the psyche. But in the dream, the forms are quirked by the peculiar troubles of the dreamer, whereas in myth the problems and solutions sown are directly valid for all mankind"

—Joseph Campbell, *The Hero With a Thousand Faces*

"I want to hold the hand inside you
I want to take a breath that's true
I look to you and I see nothing
I look to you to see the truth
You live your life
You go in shadows
You'll come apart and you'll go blind
Some kind of night into your darkness
Colors your eyes with what's not there..."

—Hope Sandoval, Fade Without You

# Chapter One

### FEVER

Wrapped tightly in soft blankets that contained her trembling, Elise considered herself a cocoon. She spied subtle white butterflies circling overhead. One landed on her nose and spoke, "Open your eyes, Elise." What a sweet voice, she thought, like a song. She tried to open her heavy lids, but the butterflies sat on her lashes, a blur of thick fur, their bodies brown and soft as cattail tips. "Open your eyes," they insisted. She trembled again, sending a thawing ache through her limbs. Butterflies scattered and she opened her eyes. Her mother's face hovered over her, eyebrows furrowed with worry.

Elise could barely remember the events that lead up to being sick. She remembered playing with Leah and then there was no Leah. She remembered playing with June and then there was no June. She was fighting with her mother and then she wasn't. Everything came and went and nothing held still.

A hand trailed ahead of her, a wide, strong and open palm that moved forward as she moved forward. Her own small palm stretched to catch it. Her fingertips nearly to his fingertips, a light shining between them. If only she could hold still long enough, she thought, she might be able to catch up to his grasp.

When her temperature reached 104 degrees, her

mother called the doctor. Barbara's voice strained to remain calm, repeating, *ahuh, ahuh*, as she scribbled on a sheet of paper. The pencil scratching blared into Elise's ear making her head throb like it might explode. Elise wanted her to stop but could not speak. There was a record playing in the distance, an old needle scratching on dusty vinyl. It was her favorite album, Free to Be You and Me, repeating, skipping, *take my hand come with me where the children are free take my hand come with me and we'll live in a land where the river runs free in a land through the green country in a land where the horses run free.* Scratching like the teeth of a saw against a tree. Elise could see the tree perfectly, ripe with red fruit. She wanted to stop the sawing, but there was no saw.

Water thundered from the faucet where her mother filled the bath. Horse hooves pounding through green fields. Her mother pounding on the ice cube tray to empty it into the tub. She lifted Elise as if she were a baby and for a moment she was soft in her mother's arms, safe against her breast before she was dropped suddenly into the cold. Her eyes shot open to the bright bathroom light, the yellow and white tiles, the white butterflies lining the shower curtain, perched on yellow flowers. Barbara held her down so she could not leap from the cold and she saw her mother's red eyes trying to keep her in, struggling to keep her contained.

In the field of horses, she could float above the small brown houses, the surrounding mountains, daisies and yarrow, white butterflies.

Her mother's words drifted in with the breeze. "Drink this," Elise drank in the echo of familiar sentences. They tasted of orange juice and dirt. "Drink more." Elise opened her eyes to find her mother perched on the ledge of the tub. Her head hung low and resting in her hands.

"Mom?" Elise said, her voice gruff.

"Sweetie," Barbara said, lifting her head, wiping her cheeks with the back of her shirt sleeve. "How are you feeling?" Her eyes were lined with dark circles.

"Was Daddy here?"

"Who?"

"I thought I saw Daddy."

"No, Sweetheart, you must have been dreaming. No one was here but me"

But Elise was sure that she was wrong. Her father was there in the field, shrouded in light and she was chasing him close behind. It was perfectly clear like the ringing of the telephone in the distance rumbling toward her, the sound pulling her apart from her dream, but she could not let go, she refused to let go. She could almost reach his hand, but it was a different hand, a little girl's hand. The girl was smiling at her, beckoning her.

Somewhere, her mother's voice begged her to return and the space around her echoed with sounds of crying, a din like coyotes above the field where the horses were grazing, where the little girl ran ahead to the apple tree, pulling her forward. She ran and ran, white butterflies following close behind.

# Chapter Two

## Early Summer

The wind funneled through the mouth of the canyon and slipped between Tree's branches, carrying the scent of wild iris. Tree listened. The mountain wind from the east did not have much to say, whispering of those things that occur above treeline—elks trumpeting, coyote pups leaving the den, and the faint whisper of a mountain lion stalking a marmot.

The screen door creaked open and slammed behind Woman and Little Girl, who turned their faces up to the sun. Little Girl wore gossamer wings and scarves flung over her purple dress. Woman wore a green gown, beaded necklaces and a paper crown. Tree half-expected them to get in the car and drive away to whatever fancy occasion they were attending, but they rarely ventured anywhere other than by foot down the road to the forest. They occupied that old house fully, encompassing its insides with a wide scale of human emotions. So much so that when they exited the adobe walls, the house seemed to sink just slightly, like an exhale.

Woman and Little Girl made their way down the stone path through the field blooming with daisies and goldenrod, past Tree, who bowed indistinctly in greeting, and to the river high with snow melt. Tree had been listening to the river all night as it picked up boulders along its banks and crashed them against felled tree trunks and river rocks. The two lean bodies, one small and one big, stood just at the edge of the rushing water. Woman dipped her toes into the current and pulled back with a screech.

Tree's root hairs, always reaching toward the river, sucked in the fresh cold waters and passed them through sapwood to the greening leaves above. Tree remained the last of a great orchard of fruit trees, now long gone, decayed and chopped down for firewood. The man who planted it died a long time ago. His great grandchildren built the house on the hill. Many people gathered around to help, digging up the clay and laying it into brick molds, stacking them until walls grew from the ground. Lodgepole pines from the mountaintop were floated down the river to construct strong *vigas* for the ceiling.

Eventually, the sounds of horse hooves on dirt lanes diminished, replaced by the faint scent of exhaust brought in by the west wind. The west wind struggled to describe the machines that made the fumes, the way they created their own power to move forward. Tree was fascinated with the idea of motion. When a car finally pulled into the driveway at the top of the hill, Tree witnessed the awesome commotion first-hand. The car grumbled and gurgled, spat and spewed, smoke pumping out of its backside. Tree felt simultaneously disgusted by the foul smell and enchanted by the undeniable force.

Soon after, the west wind brought scents of tar and freshly milled lumber. The town grew, bringing shops, new homes and roads, while the ranches surrounding Tree remained mostly the same. Cowboys drove cattle and baled hay. Women tended to their families and grew food for the table—peaches, lentils, *havas*, corn, plums, and squash. The river bustled with fresh trout for the taking. Two nights and one day a week, the families—children trailing behind in white dresses and dress shirts while parents scolded them to stay out of mud puddles—visited the tiny church at the end of the road. The world seemed to go quiet but for the sounds of hushed chanting that filled the air.

When the people who built the house died, their children lived in the house with their children and their children's children. Tree was taken care of—sun-browned hands pruning, wide hands thinning, hard hands harvesting. Small gullies were dug up near Tree, an irrigation system that took water from the river to water the crops and return it to the river when done. Tree understood then that it was necessary—its apples were made into cider or sauce, butter or jam, to feed the hands that would come again in the spring.

Tree witnessed its small world populate. All around, land was squared off into parcels, tenuous trailers erected on tiny lots. Pastures turned into yards. Eventually, only small herds of cows and horses remained.

Tree was confused when, seasons later, the west wind delivered more news—the people were leaving. "But it seems like they've just arrived!" Tree said, "Why would they leave?"

"In town, the shops are closing down," the west wind reported, "and houses are abandoned." The wind warned of a mass movement toward something called the city, but it could not carry a whiff to help Tree understand.

When they came with chainsaws, Tree feared for its life, but they never felled it like they did the others—

decayed, thirsty and dry. Instead, they left Tree there in the vast open field with only the moody river for company. They left nothing behind, not even stumps. Then, the family packed up their belongings and piled them into their truck, leaving the house and Tree alone.

The burden of the domestic tree, birthed and cared for by humans, it relied on them and wished to be near them. It gave back all that it had—shade, blossoms and fruit. Tree hoped for a new family to move in and keep it company, but the house sat for a very long time, the low windows seemed to droop with fatigue and the roof lost its will to stay atop. The fallow land overgrew with tall grasses, wildflowers and berries. Tree missed the soft hum of human lives surrounding it.

For one summer, just a moment amongst the years, a small, unusual tribe of people took over the house on the hill. They moved together in a pod with no regard for clothes, often shoeless and naked from the waist up. Smoke seeped from their lips as they squinted at the sun and howled at the moon. In constant awe, Tree watched them drifting about in a dreamy state, bodies and arms undulating to loud electric music blasting out of walls. The little house looked as if it might implode or tip over from the ecstatic ruckus.

One day, mid-summer, the sun high in the sky, the people held hands in a circle and danced around Tree. Tree raised its limbs as tall as it could, both to protect and to mimic the dancers. They laughed and skipped and Tree belonged again. But that night, their bonfire burned until morning, and when the wind picked up at dawn, Tree, who had not felt a drop of rain in several weeks, dodged and darted the tiny embers that floated its way.

One piece of red drifting ash landed on the tip of Tree's highest leaf. It felt a singe and moved back and forth in an attempt to stop the pain, which only made it worse. Tree shut down. Comatose, it did not awaken until nightfall. Cautiously returning to consciousness, Tree had not burned down, only lost some foliage, a small branch or two, endured some scars. Tree grew very little fruit that year.

A couple of men came to check on the house and were enraged to discover the naked bodies hanging over porch railings and wood piles while the house deteriorated into a filthy shambles. They evicted the tribe immediately, tossing their few possessions into their van and dragging them away by their long hair. When they left, the valley seemed more silent than ever.

Many more seasons passed until one day, Tree spotted people that it had never seen before. They circled the house once or twice, discussing its sorry skeleton. Little Girl wandered off and called back to Woman to see the colors of flowers she found. Woman laughed, surprising Tree. It had been a long while since it had heard such rich laughter, and something in the echo of her cackle struck ancient rungs in its timber. Tree stood up taller, reached higher, expanded its blossom tips to the cloudless sky.

"Look, Julia, a whole field of beautiful flowers for us to run through!" Woman exclaimed. "We can collect them and put them in a vase, keep them on every table of the house. What do you think?" Little Girl nodded eagerly. Woman continued, "We'll press them into books and during long winters, take them out to admire them and call up their fairy spirits." Little Girl giggled, a high pitched trill, and jumped up and down. Woman swung her around. Tree knew then that it was no longer alone.

The house was uplifted. A new green roof was put on, the windows were replaced with larger, jollier windows and the grass was cut, but not the field; they never touched a blade to the field. Once the structure was ready, the people began to move their belongings in—books, plates and chairs. Woman and Little Girl discovered Tree.

"Look, Mama, a big tree."

"I wonder what kind it is? Maybe it will have flowers and fruit."

Tree wanted to tell them right away that it was an apple tree, but it was best to let the secret unfold. Little Girl reached up for a branch and Woman lifted her so she could grasp Tree's shortest limb. Tree held to Little Girl strongly. She began to swing, slightly.

"A trapeze artist! In a big circus, traveling through Africa and exotic lands. And I am a lion tamer."

Dog lifted his leg to Tree's base and ran to Woman, jumping up to meet her raised arms. Tree did not care for Dog.

"I want to be lion t'mer, too. Help down." Woman helped Little Girl jump from Tree and she fell to the ground in a crouch. She roared and wrapped her arms around Dog's ribbed back.

"And I am a lion, RAWR!"

They ran off with Dog, a small pride of lions, stalking their prey in the wild savannah.

Two summers had passed since then. Tree watched as Woman and Little Girl played in the river, ankle deep in numbing cold waters, their gowns pulled in the current.

"Let's go to the mermaid ball and put the prince under a spell. We'll turn him into a..."

"A bear," said Little Girl, "a big white polar bear."

They set off down the river waving sticks with ribbons tied to the ends, stomping and singing about mermaids and bears. Soon, they were running back from the west holding their dresses up over their knees. Dog chased them, as it chased helpless squirrels up to Tree's highest branches, with a pounce and quick pursuit. Little Girl yelled, "The polar bear is after us now! Let's get to the fairy cave!"

Tree proudly played the role of the fairy cave as it felt the little heaving breaths of its people leaning up against its trunk. Tree raised its roots to meet them.

Woman pulled lollipops from a hidden pocket inside her dress and they sat together sucking on them silently for a while until Tree's shade shifted and they picked up their skirts and headed back up to the house plucking dandelions along the way.

Tree listened to the music playing from inside, catching the shadows of people twirling within.

That night, Tree noticed something new seep through its skins, a barely noticeable blip, a sour taste in the air. At first, it was concerned that there might be a fire in the south forest, but it did not sense smoke so much as the kicking up of dust and rock. For three days, the change lingered and Tree began to think that it might be something more permanent, the way its breath never felt quite as deep after the first scents of exhaust remained. The west wind said nothing but the flooding of forests, the east wind only noted that children did not return to school. Tree waited for the south wind, a rare and private air stream, to deliver word. When it finally visited, the south wind spoke of new construction on the other side of the canyon wall. Old forest land had been dug up for pipes and concrete. Giant vehicles toiled day and night to break up the rocky clay earth.

How many more would they destroy? Tree worried. How much more can they pave over? Humans were a complete mystery to Tree. They were so smart, so innovative, and yet they did not understand something as simple as breath; the symbiotic life between humans and trees, one infinite exhale.

As if to soothe it, Little Girl meandered down the hill to Tree in the faint light of dawn. Tree shook its branches with understated excitement, mimicking a soft breeze. Head down, she did not notice.

Little Girl crawled to the lowest part of Tree's base and pulled back a small patch of turf. Tree felt her burrowing within its roots. She had a hiding spot in the moist earth there. Tree felt the electricity of crumpled tin and the dampness of paper like bones. It felt queasy with the stale taste of colored plastic. Little Girl pulled out the old tin box and opened it. She lined up the little toy contents in a row along the ridge of Tree's tallest root and marched them until they each leaped two at a time to the soft soil below.

She sang a song in her sweet little voice. Tree could only hear a few words, "bird," "laugh," "girl." Dog came over to lie by Little Girl and she responded by roughly hugging his head. For the moment, Tree, Little Girl and Dog played peacefully by the river bed, ignoring the clanking and crunching in the distance.

# Chapter Three

## JESUS

Julia danced to the sound of a million trumpets, slowly at first, swaying from side to side with a slight lift of her foot, but rapidly accelerating to more vigorous leaps, bouncing off the ottoman and lounge chair as her imagined song reached a crescendo and ended. She curtsied to her applauding toys lined up on the couch. Farley barked to be let in. Julia ran to the door and opened it. "Dance with me, Fa'ley," but he only wanted a biscuit.

Mama was sweating over the hot stove, finishing up some rhubarb jelly to can for winter. Julia was not allowed in the kitchen while Mama cooked, and lingered close in the large doorway. She watched as Mama referred back to recipes and canning directions strewn across the counter top beside jars, lids and fresh towels. Between each movement, Mama took a swig of her wine.

Mama had never canned before, but she decided that this year she would not let anything go to waste. After more than two years in the country, she still struggled to work in rhythm with the seasons. Julia had grown tired of all the rhubarb recipes Mama had conjured up—rhubarb pork sauce, rhubarb pie, rhubarb tarts, rhubarb muffins. If she had to taste rhubarb one more time, she told her she'd gag. Mama comforted Julia, "By mid-winter, we will gladly open a jar of jelly to smell spring."

Even with the window open and the fan on, the house remained hot. A great rumbling noise grew from the distance and, suddenly upon them, stuttered and crackled, throwing up rocks. Julia had once asked Mama about the big trucks that passed throughout the day. She wondered when they would stop coming, since Mama had locked the front gate to the yard, worried that Julia might traipse into the road and be hit by a giant rubber tire. She also wanted to know about the bulldozers, how they worked, and the backhoes, how much they could shovel in one scoop. Mama would never take her to see them.

"Why? Because they're tearing apart the mountain, that's why. And what will follow them will only be worse; traffic, commuters, and big boxes." Mama complained over the steaming stove top, addressing an invisible crowd of people, the ones always questioning her motives. She paused and the expression on her face transformed from wrath to resolution. "I have a great idea," Mama said squatting down wide-eyed beside her, the smell of wine on her breath. Julia loved Mama's ideas. She jumped up and down, "What is it? What is it?"

"Let's pretend we are pioneers. You know, like in the old days, and we are homesteading. We'll rough it and live off the land."

Julia didn't understand what pioneer meant, but she thought it would be fun to live off the land. She imagined it might involve floating up to the sky like the time they rode on the black bird's back, the one who complained the whole time about the extra weight while Julia and Mama kept their heads low, hunkered behind feathers to block out the wind. Mama stopped washing the dish she had soaped up, went to the metal box on the wall and flicked the master switch. The fan came to a stop. The hum disappeared. The home hushed. She thought she heard it sigh.

"Isn't that better?" Mama said. Julia nodded.

Mama turned to finish the dishes. The water turned into a trickle and stopped. "The pump," she mumbled. Then, she laughed, "Isn't this silly?"

"Now what, Mama?"

"Hm. We should build a fire and roast some veggies on a stick. Let's go forage for vegetables in the wilds of our garden." She took Julia's little hand in hers and guided her into the front yard. Mama slipped on gloves and opened the garden gate. Julia loved to play in the garden. She learned young where she could step and where she could not. This year, Mama gave her her own bed to tend and allowed her to plant anything she wanted. She sowed six carrots, one pumpkin plant, five sun flowers and all the *hava* beans she had. Juanita, her neighbor, gave Mama the *hava* beans and told her they were very special, passed down from her grandmother. Mama didn't know what *havas* were, so she gave them all to Julia.

Each year, Mama struggled with the garden, putting her entire heart and back into making it grow, hoping that year would be better than the last and each year, by July, Julia found her hunched beside her beds crying over the few shoots that actually appeared. Still early in the season, Mama examined her sparse bed of chard, kale and romaine and sighed. She shook her head, "Well, it will have to do." Julia admired her own bed, "Look, Mama. Look at my *hava* plants, they're already coming up big." Mama laughed with exasperation.

Julia helped Mama prepare a salad for dinner. After the sun went down, Mama lit an old gas lamp and they read books in the dim light, until Julia fell asleep in a pile of blankets on the living room floor. Mama paced the house at night like a restless ghost. Whenever Julia woke up in the middle of the night to use the potty, Mama greeted her with such enthusiasm that Julia became confused as to whether it was late or early.

Julia awoke to the sun shining into her eyes. There were no curtains in the living room. She called out for Mama and searched the empty house. She peered out the windows until she spotted Mama's golden hair glinting with new sun. Julia wrapped herself in a blanket and went outside to join her, frying eggs over the fire on a grill she fashioned from an old iron table top. The sun had not yet burned off the chill of night. She sat on a rock, still hazy with sleep. Farley came over and licked her face. She swatted him away.

"Mornin' Pumpkin, how did you sleep?"

"Good," Julia replied though she had a hazy feeling from the remnants of a bad dream, something like falling. "Are we still playing pioneer ladies?"

"Oh yeah, we got a fire going and a yummy breakfast... Maybe we're more like cowboys camping out on the range."

"I like cowboys." Julia knew about cowboys from her books. She had one called, "The Little Cowboy," about a boy who lived by himself with his horses and, on occasion, helped the sheriff save the town from bad guys. She couldn't remember any part of the book where he fried eggs over a campfire.

"Cowgirls it is then. And Farley can be our trusty horse."

"Farley's not a horse. He's a dog."

"Is that so? He sure does smell like a horse. Don't you, Farley?"

Farley perked up his ears and wagged his tail. "You're stinky, Farley," Julia added. Farley jumped onto his feet. "P.U.," she laughed.

After eggs, they went to work in the garden. They filled buckets with water from the river and carried it through the field and up the hill to the seedlings. Julia thought being a cowgirl may be more work than fun. She wanted milk. Inside, Mama opened the fridge and a foul smell spilled out. She opened the milk carton and took a sniff, then pulled away quickly. "Sorry, Pumpkin, the milk is bad."

"But I want milk," Julia whined.

"Well, we could go milk a cow, I guess, but we'd have to go find one first. Shouldn't be too hard."

"I don't want to milk a cow! I want milk now!" Julia raised her voice and stomped her feet.

"I think it's nap time for you, little miss."

"I don't want to take a nap. I'm not tired."

"Is that why you are whining so much?"

"I'm not whining!"

"Don't you yell at me."

"Please, Mama, I don't want to nap."

"Come on, I'll tell you a story." Julia loved Mama's stories so she conceded to a nap. Mama laid beside her and spun a long tale until her words became dreams.

\*\*\*

Julia woke to the sound of Juanita, in the living room, talking to Mama about the *posole* she had brought over for them. Juanita always came over with food with names like *tamales* and *gorditas*. Most of the time Juanita's food was too spicy for Julia, but she always liked to try it.

One day when they first moved into their house, Juanita asked Mama to drive her to the hospital because she had bad stomach pains. Mama didn't like to go anywhere, especially hospitals, but Juanita had nobody else to take her and she worried that it might be serious. So, she drove her and waited all day for her to get admitted while Julia colored every page in the hospital coloring book. She liked the pictures of doctors with their funny stethoscopes helping people lying in bed or the ambulance,which she colored purple, even though she knew they were white. Juanita ended up being fine. She had dyspepsia, which Mama said was a fancy word for having a big air bubble in your belly that won't come out, or a fart. Julia laughed at this, but Mama said it wasn't funny. After that, Mama sometimes didn't answer the door when Juanita knocked. Instead, she hid inside and waited until Juanita left. Julia pretended it was a game, like peek-a-boo.

Julia hid behind Mama's leg.

"How are you *m'jita*? You look pretty today," Juanita said.

"I'm a cowgirl," Julia informed her.

"Oh, a cowgirl. Lucky you."

Mama smiled, "It's a little game we're playing. We turned off the electricity and we're pretending to be homesteaders."

"Really? My mother didn't have no electricity when

she was a little girl. She used to grow all kinds of things; lentils, *havas*, *calabacitas*..."

"I have *havas*." Julia interjected.

"Oh, you do? Do you like *calabacitas*?"

"I like *calabacitas*," she said even though she wasn't sure what that was.

"You do? Well, I'll bring you some." Juanita turned to Mama, "She's so cute."

"Do you want to see my room?" Julia asked.

"Oh no, I have to get home. It's dark in here, no?"

"Is it?" Mama said.

"Do you have water, Elise? How are you going to wash without water?"

"We get it from the river."

"Eeh, but it's so cold."

"We're fine, Juanita."

"*Bueno*. Bye, bye *m'jita*."

"Bye," Julia called.

Mama stood in the doorway and watched Juanita's stout body move farther away. She mumbled to the screen door, "Why does she always have to act like she's my mother? I didn't ask her to come over here and give me food or her guilt trips. We're doing just fine, right, Pumpkin?" Julia nodded her head as convincingly as she could. Mama continued, "We have everything we need here. We have each other. That's all that matters, right?" Again, Julia nodded, but Mama didn't look at her. Her questions hovered in the air of the darkened room. She sat down at the kitchen table with a bottle and a glass of wine that she sipped from between breaths. Julia examined Mama's face, the way her eyelids became heavy and her mouth hung open as if her whole face fell under the weight of a rotten pumpkin. Julia tried to stir her, "Let's go play cowgirls, Mama."

"Not now, baby. Mama needs a little quiet time. Why don't you go play outside with Farley."

Mama once told her that, when she was a little baby, she kept her up all night with her crying, that she didn't have a full night's rest for over a year. That's why Julia thought Mama was tired, because she took all that sleep from her.

Julia sat at the table beside Mama and glanced out the window to try to find what Mama was looking at, but there was just an old lilac tree and some grass. Soon, Julia grew bored and went outside to visit her apple tree.

There was something different about her tree today. She had noticed it once or twice before—when Mama was having quiet time, Tree grew quiet too. Its leaves turned inward and it seemed to slouch, as if it were weighted by the hovering gray clouds. Mama had told her about fairies that lived in trees called dryads, and Julia felt sure that Tree had one of those in it—a girl, a beautiful fairy princess trapped in the tree by a wicked witch. Mama must have been under the same witch's spell. They were connected by the hex, bound to live in a nether world, swinging back and forth between happy and sad. Considering how she might break the spell, Julia began pulling at clovers and dandelion heads. She spoke magic elfin words, while smashing the plants between her palms.

Once the potion was thoroughly pulverized and contained in a small rock pile vessel to simmer, Julia pulled out the treasure box she kept hidden beneath Tree's roots. She removed each toy one by one and lined them up around the potion to assist with the cooking. She looked up at the house, dark inside, like nighttime.

In the near distance stood a mountain that she liked to look at while playing with Tree. She felt like it belonged to her. It towered near and watched over things and she waved to it and said hello.

By the end of the day, Mama still had not moved. Julia gathered up her potion and went back inside. She flipped the switch, but the lights did not come on. In the dimming light, she managed to help herself to dinner—crackers from the pantry and a brown banana. She climbed into Mama's lap. Mama petted her hair, her fingers like air. "Here, Mama, open your hand." Mama turned her hand upward and Julia put her potion of crushed weeds inside it, pressing firmly into her palm. "Now, eat it up." Mama played along and brought the strange mixture up to her mouth, going through the motions of pretending to chew. "Yum," she said softly.

"Mama," Julia whispered, "Can I ask you something?" She had been thinking about something for a long time but never seemed able to get the words right. Mama grunted, which Julia took to be a yes. "Where do you go when you are quiet like that?"

"I'm right here." Her voice sounded tired and her eyes did not look directly at Julia.

"I mean, do you go somewhere else, in your head or something?" Julia wished for more words —big, important ones like adults knew how to use.

"I get lost a little, my soul wanders off."

"What's a soul?"

"It's the thing about you that you can't see or hear or feel. Mama's tired, Pumpkin. Go get ready for bed."

Julia used the potty, but when she flushed it, nothing happened. The yellow water just sat there, so she closed the lid. Then, she climbed into bed with her clothes still on and made a spot for herself among the toys and books. She thought about things she could not see or hear or feel. There was the ghost that she and Mama once spent all afternoon tracking through the forest and there were the little people who lived under the polka-dot mushrooms. But neither of them were souls. Julia drifted to sleep in search of invisible things.

She woke up to the sound of Mama in the kitchen cursing.

"There's no fucking food in this house."

Mama sat back down at the table with a cup of black coffee and stared out the window. Julia's empty stomach growled. She went outside and threw rocks over the garden fence.

"Watcha doin' *m'jita*?"

Julia turned around quickly. She hadn't noticed Juanita coming up the driveway, her old legs making great efforts to take small strides.

"Throwing rocks."

"Oh. Where's your mama? I brought you some *calabacita* stew. I made it for you because you said you liked it."

"Thank you."

"So polite! Is your Mama inside?"

"Yeah."

"What's she doing?"

"She's just sitting."

"Oh. Is she working?"

"No."

"Oh well, I don't want to bother her. How 'bout I just leave this pot here and you let her know I dropped it off, okay?"

"Do you want to throw rocks?"

"Oh no, *m'jita*, I've got to get home."

"Do you like bulldozers?"

"Oh. I guess so."

"I saw one."

"Oh yes. They're building that road for the development. They're putting in a whole lot of houses on the other side of the ridge there." Juanita pointed toward the canyon wall. "A bunch more people are going to move in here. I remember when no one but my family lived here. It was beautiful then. I don't know what's going to happen now..." They stared up at the hillside as if waiting for something to happen.

"Are there going to be kids there?"

"Oh, you poor thing. You must be lonely here in this dark house."

"I've got Mama."

"*Bueno*," Juanita said, "Jesus will look out for you *m'jita*," and she touched her on the head. As she walked off she said, "Tell your mama to bring the pot back when you are done."

Julia could not carry the pot, so she told Mama about it. Mama just nodded, "That's nice, Pumpkin."

Julia got a spoon from the drawer and brought it outside. She ate the stew from the pot and discovered that she did like *calabacitas*. She went inside to ask Mama, "Mama, who's Jesus?"

"What?" Mama turned to face her as if Julia had spoken the magic word to break the spell, abracadabra, the prince's kiss.

"Who is Jesus?"

"Where did you hear that?" Her voice strained, high pitched and quick.

"From Juanita. I told you she was here. She brought us cala'citas. It's good. I like it."

Mama stood up and looked around the room as if lost—the adobe walls that held them in, the old wood table with chipping paint, the refrigerator that had not moaned or hummed in two days.

Mama grabbed Julia's hand and began to stride down the road toward Juanita's house. Julia did not have shoes on and had trouble keeping up. "Mama, hold me, hold me." She raised her arms and jumped in front of Mama's long legs until Mama lifted her up, never breaking stride. Farley met up with them along the road where he was digging up dirt, trying to outsmart a field mouse. They walked past Mr. Maestas' horses, past the old house missing the back wall so that you could see inside like looking at someone naked, and past the hay field before finally getting to the end of Juanita's driveway.

Juanita lived alone with no car and no phone, but she had five dogs that barked at visitors and made a special ruckus for Farley. Sometimes, she mentioned her daughter who lived in another state, but Julia never saw her visit. One time, Julia went inside Juanita's house, which was dark and cold, and Juanita showed her where she used to sleep when she was a little girl growing up there. Julia had a hard time imagining Juanita as a little girl. She wondered if they would have been friends.

Mama waited at the end of the driveway until Juanita called the dogs off. Juanita waved. Julia avoided looking at her and buried her face in Mama's shoulder, afraid Juanita would be mad at her for telling.

"Hello, Elise," Juanita said, still smiling.

"What are you telling my daughter about Jesus?"

"Huh? Nothing."

"Then why did she ask me who Jesus was?"

Juanita looked at Julia. Julia hid her face.

"I just told her that Jesus would watch out for her."

"Well, I don't need you pushing your religious beliefs on my daughter."

"I'm not trying to tell nothing to nobody. I just see that the girl is lonely, that's all."

"Well, she has me and that's all she needs. I watch over her, not your Jesus. I'm the only one that watches over her and Jesus never did shit for me."

From a small crack between her hair and Mama's shirt, Julia saw Juanita's eyes grow big. Mama turned quickly and trotted away. Julia wanted to wave goodbye, but feared Mama might notice.

When they reached the yard, Mama set her down to walk on her own again. "I have an idea," she said. Julia looked at Juanita's pot sitting on the rock near the garden fence. Mama disappeared in the tangle of willow trees and began tossing out branches. Julia could hear the sound of them cracking over her knee. Then, she came out of the trees and began sticking the ends of the branches into the soft springy soil along the river, placing them in a circle. Julia watched quietly from a distance.

Mama disappeared into the house and came back with twine and a blanket. She tied the tops of the branches together and then wrapped them with a blanket as if throwing a shawl over someone's hunched shoulders. She stood back to admire her work, "There," she said.

Julia shuffled closer, "What is it?"

"A teepee."

"What's a teepee?"

"It's a house like the Indians used to live in. They would set it up and take it down when they moved their hunting grounds with the seasons. They never left a trace. Of course, theirs were covered with animal hides instead of blankets."

Mama pulled back the corner of the blanket and Julia saw that it made a door. Mama crawled in first and beckoned her to follow. She climbed in to the soft circular abode and sat in the grass.

"Let's pretend we're Indians," Mama said.

"How do we do that?"

"We can sing songs and tell stories."

"Okay."

Mama opened her arms wide as if to let the story in and Julia noticed that her arms made spooky shadows against the teepee walls. Mama's voice, deep and hushed, filled the tiny cavern.

*Once upon a time, a young woman named Eliza lived alone in a small cabin with her cat in the middle of a very large forest in the mountains far, far away. Her father had left the cabin to her when he died a few years before, and so she lived in it to remember him by and because she had nowhere else to go. Every day, Eliza took long walks through the woods by herself. With her head hung low and her feet dragging behind her, she wished she knew the joy she used to feel when her father was still alive.*

*One day, she awoke as usual, washed and dressed, ate*

*breakfast, fed her cat and opened the creaky wooden door to take her daily walk. But on this day, someone had laid a golden gown delicately at the foot of her doorstep. Eliza's mouth fell open and her eyes widened as she took in the sight of the beautiful dress. It glimmered and shone with each sunbeam that made its way through the waving branches of the forest canopy. Eliza grazed the gown with her fingertips and it felt smooth as silk, soft as cashmere. She felt reserved about trying it on, but, as if responding to her hesitation, there was a note attached that read: For Eliza.*

*She only wondered for a moment who it could be from. She scanned the woods for any sign of a human and then rushed the gown inside. In the dimly lit cabin, she could better see the iridescent glow that surrounded the dress and she was sure it had to be enchanted. Immediately, she put it on and her whole world began to glow, just like the dress itself. Her cabin filled with light and color that she had never noticed before. She swung open the door and outside the sun shone radiant against the green glade, shimmering river and brushed bark. The air felt cool and soothing. She smelled the flowers in bloom as if she was swimming in perfume.*

*As she walked, she barely touched upon the ground. Smiling, like she had not done in years, she did not once contemplate her sorrow or wish to be someone else or somewhere else. The whole day passed like that in the forest, Eliza absorbing the world anew.*

*When the sun set over the mountains like an explosion of downy jewels, Eliza returned home to her cabin, ate a delectable meal of potatoes and greens and readied herself for bed. When the dress fell to the floor around her feet, the world darkened around her. The walls of her cabin pushed in toward the center of the room and the ceiling lowered. With each step she took toward her bed, she sunk into the wood floor. Her bed was cold as a stone slab. Her blankets weighed down on her fragile frame so that she felt as if she were descending into the ground.*

*In the morning, Eliza felt anxious to put her enchanted gown back on. She dragged her heavy body out of bed and pulled the dress over her.*

*"Ahhhh," she said as if she had just found water in a sandy desert. The dress filled her up from head to toe with light and joy such that she no longer wished to walk, but instead waltzed her way through the forest gathering flowers, ripe berries and nuts. For a moment, she thought she spotted a strange little man spying on her from behind an aspen, but when she opened her mouth to say hello, a song came out instead. The man disappeared. She continued, through the woods, floating and harmonizing with the birds.*

*She returned home to get ready for bed. This time, when the dress fell to the ground, so did Eliza. Her body fell to the floor like a puddle of fabric and she struggled to take a breath. Dragging her pile of skin into bed, she remained in the awkward position she landed there in. So tired, her eyelids weighted down with somber sleep. She drifted into slumber hoping she would feel better in the morning.*

*Eliza had a dream. The little man that she had spotted in the forest earlier that day sat in her room beside her bed beckoning her to put the dress back on. "The dress will make everything better," he said in a wicked little voice.*

*Her eyes tried to stay focused on the man. She was immediately wary of him. He could not have been more than two feet tall and below his stout torso were two sticks of leg, which bent awkwardly under his weight. He wore a blue suit and a bushy red beard. Deep wrinkles surrounded the oddest green color for pupils that winked with impish glee.*

*Nevertheless, Eliza wanted to feel better and so she put on the dress. But instead of the joy she felt before, she felt horror as she watched the skin of her arms turn to muslin cloth. She reached up to feel her face before losing sensation in her fingertips and saw her hair turn to yarn. Her eyes turned to buttons and everything went blank. Just before she awoke, she saw her father, calling to her from deep in the woods.*

*Eliza opened her eyes. Her body was damp with sweat and still weak. The dream was so fresh and vivid in her mind, she thought it might have been real, but her house remained empty and the dress laid crumpled in a pile on the floor.*

*She had trouble lifting her head, swinging her body out of bed and onto the floor. She knew the dress would hold her up, but she remembered what happened to her in the dream when she put it on. Eliza reached for a pair of scissors from her bedside table. They were heavy and cold in her palm. Lying on her back, she opened the scissors against the dress like teeth ready to take a bite. Just then, the little man appeared from behind the cook stove dressed in a funny purple suit.*

*"Stop!" he yelled in his peculiar voice, "Don't!"*

*Eliza let her arms fall back to the ground with a heavy sigh. "Why not?"*

*"Please, I am begging you."*

*"Then give me back my bones," Eliza murmured.*

*"I cannot. It is too late for that. They are gone."*

*"Where are they?"*

*The little man looked away. Eliza reached for the scissors again.*

"Okay. I will tell you," he said. "They are buried, beneath the old tree, at the forest's edge."

"But, how will I get there?"

"The dress will make everything better," he said.

*Eliza recognized his words from her dream and knew that the dress would only take more from her.* "No," *she said,* "Take back the dress. I only want my bones." *The little man swiped the dress from her diminished grip and disappeared out the window.*

*Eliza knew she could barely walk and it would take too long and be too difficult to slither there. She rolled her body out the door, down the hill and into the river. She let her body and head be submerged in the cold water before returning afloat. She sunk and rose with the rushing rapids releasing and flowing, floating downstream to the forest's edge. When she spotted the old tree, she held to a log protruding from the sandy bank with all her remaining strength and rolled herself onto land. She lay down beneath the tree exhausted and cried.*

*Tired from the journey, she soon fell asleep. She dreamed that the tree's roots pulled her down beneath the soil, damp and dark. She watched the plump red earthworms dig through rich brown granules and tiny stones while the tree roots replaced each bone one by one back to her body before lifting her back to the earth's surface. Then the tree asked her for something in return for her bones. After some negotiation, she agreed to give the tree her voice. Her father stood off to the right smiling and nodding. She stepped closer and reached for him.*

*She awoke with her arms outstretched. She pulled*

*them back to her body and they felt light and sure, balanced with sturdy bones. She stood and hugged the old tree, no longer animated, but stoic and still. She had a long hike back to the cabin but she felt wonderful to be whole again. Everything became clear to her now like the cloudless sky. She even skipped part of the way home.*

*When she walked in the door, she called to her cat, but nothing came out of her throat but breath. She had surrendered her voice to the tree in exchange for her bones. Many years would pass before she questioned if she made the right choice.*

When the pause lingered long enough for Julia to realize the story had finished, she was disappointed. She never wanted a story to end.

Mama turned her head up slowly and gazed out the opening at the top of the teepee. Julia placed her head in Mama's lap and followed her stare out the teepee's tip to the small sight of sky. She closed her eyes and imagined that she was an Indian princess living in the cotton-tail clouds with her tribe to protect her.

# Chapter Four

### Nana

Julia was reaching for a granola bar in the basket on the table when she heard a knock on the door. Mama was sitting at the table, staring out the window.

"There's a knock, Mama."

Mama did not move. Julia wondered what to do. No one ever knocked on their door except for Juanita sometimes, but Juanita had not been back since Mama yelled at her for mentioning Jesus. The knock came again, louder. Julia peeked out the window. It had been raining since the early hours of the day. The windows were foggy and splattered with drops. She saw a red and shiny car. She could not see the person at the door. The knock came again and Julia decided there was nothing else to do but open the door. She struggled with the knob at eye level. Using both hands, she twisted it roughly in either direction until it gave way. The woman waiting in the rain turned to her and smiled. "Julia! Look at you! You've gotten so big. Do you remember me? I haven't seen you in over two years."

Julia did not remember the woman at the door though she seemed familiar. She was tall and broad with gray wavy hair to her shoulders and big purple-framed glasses. "Well, can I come in?" Julia nodded shyly. The woman crouched down, "You don't remember me, do you? You were so little when I saw you last. It's me, your

Grandma, Nana."

Julia's head and eyebrows lifted. She knew from books that grandmas were family and that they baked cookies and brought presents. She wanted to ask Nana if she had either of these. "Where is your mommy?" Julia looked in the direction of the kitchen.

In the kitchen, where the lights were still off, Mama began to wake from her trance. She was standing awkwardly, trying to recall where she was, when Nana entered.

"Mom? What are you doing here?"

"Don't be mad at me, Elise. I hadn't heard from you in several months. I was worried. I wanted to see my granddaughter and what you've done with the house and make sure that everything is okay. It's not right to just cut me out of your life again."

"I'm not cutting you out of my life. I've just been busy." Julia wondered what Mama meant. If she wasn't having a quiet day, as she did most often, then she played or cooked, went on walks or told stories. Julia considered that Mama might believe that she was busy being two different people, the happy one and the sad one.

"You're never too busy for your mother, Elise."

"How did you get here?"

"I flew in this morning and rented a car from the airport and drove up. It is not easy to find this place."

"How long are you staying?"

"I only have the rental car reserved for a week. That's really all I could afford. They're so expensive nowadays and..."

"Why didn't you tell me you were coming?"

"You never call me back. Besides, if I told you, would

you have let me come?"

Mama huffed and sat down, turning back to the window as if she were upset and didn't want to talk about it.

Nana turned to Julia, "Now, let me see your room. Show me around."

Julia skipped through the house. No one had ever asked to see her room before. Her mother had painted, at Julia's request, pretty green and purple flowers all over the pink walls, which made her room the prettiest one in the house. She also had shelves for all her books and a basket for all of her toys. She had a mattress on the floor covered with blankets and stuffed animals. "Oh, what a beautiful room!" Nana said, which pleased Julia.

"Will you read me this book?" Julia asked.

"I would love to," Nana said, taking off her coat and shoes and putting them neatly by the door to the room. She flicked the light switch and nothing happened. "Is the bulb out?" she asked.

"No."

"Then, where are the lights?"

"Mama turned off the electricity, so we can play cowgirls."

"That sounds fun. How long ago was that?" Nana asked suspiciously.

"Three days ago."

Nana shook her head. She walked back into the kitchen and searched the four walls until she found the metal box. She opened it and clicked the big switch on top into place. Without looking in Mama's direction, she returned to Julia's room, bumping into Julia on the way. "Let's read," she said turning on the lamp next to Julia's bed.

First coming to her knees and then awkwardly turning over onto her bottom, she sat down on the mattress. She patted the empty spot beside her and Julia eagerly curled up in the crook of her arm and listened to the lulling voice of her grandmother. When Nana tired of reading, Julia showed her her dolls and some of the toys Mama had bought for her on their monthly trips to town. Nana showed interest in everything on display, so Julia began pulling out objects tucked away at the bottom of her toy box—a broken barrette, a crayon with the wrapper peeled off, a page torn from a magazine.

"This is all so lovely, but aren't you hungry? It must be late."

Nana returned to the kitchen where Mama sat in the same position they had left her in. "Do you have any plans for dinner?" Nana asked.

Mama humphed to show that she was still mad, but did not otherwise respond. Nana opened the refrigerator and a terrible smell tumbled out. She closed it quickly, shaking her head. Going through the cabinets, she pulled out cans of food, opened them up and emptied them all into a soup pot on the stove.

"This is called Nana Soup Surprise," she said placing the bowl in front of Julia who ate it up so fast her tummy felt funny. Occasionally, Mama snorted when Nana spoke, but Nana ignored her.

At bedtime, Nana offered to tuck Julia in if she brushed her teeth and used the potty. Julia didn't know how to brush her teeth. Nana sighed deeply. Julia thought she was mad at her, but then Nana offered to help.

Nana said she was tired of reading books. Instead, she sang Julia a bedtime song. "This is one your mommy loved when she was a little girl." Julia liked to think of Mama as a little girl, listening to lullabies, happy. Just before leaving, Nana turned to Julia and asked in an adult voice, "Is mommy always like this?"

"Sometimes she plays."

"Oh, that's good."

"But mostly, she's like this."

Nana frowned and closed the door behind her.

Julia awoke to the sound of arguing outside of her room. Dragging her blanket, she hid behind the doorway to the kitchen and listened.

"Elise, I know it was difficult for you after the birth, but she's nearly five now and you need to snap out of it. You can't sleep through life. You have a little girl to take care of."

"I take good care of that little girl," Mama strained her voice, "You don't know anything about our life. You just showed up, unannounced, and now you are telling me what to do."

"Don't you think I want to be a part of your life? Do you think I enjoy being shut out by you? I helped you move and buy this house and I have kept my mouth shut to Sam about where you are. The least you can do is call me once in a while."

"Is that a threat?"

"Of course not, Elise." Nana's voice calmed. "I'm just worried about you. I want to see my granddaughter."

"Fine. You're seeing her now."

"He asks for you all the time, you know? He wants to see her. He misses you both, so much. I hate to see you do this to him."

"I can't, Mom. I'm not ready, yet. I don't want him

to see me like this. He thinks he can make everything better, and he can't."

"Maybe he can."

"No, mom, he can't. I'm all screwed up."

Julia cringed.

"Don't forget, Elise, you're the one that stole her away from him and the time is going to come when he is going to come looking. It's been two years and he has respected your space, but that's his daughter…"

"He's going to take her away from me."

"You don't know that, Elise. He still loves you, very much; he hasn't given up on you."

Nana and Mama were quiet and Julia took it as an invitation to enter. "Mama?"

"Hello, Pumpkin. You're awake."

Nana placed a plate on the table. "Here you go, Jujubean. I went out and got some eggs and bacon at the little gas station on the corner." Julia, pleased to have a new nickname, ate up the warm food. Nana turned to Mama, "There's nothing in this town. I don't know how you live here. There's just a gas station and a Catholic church, which, by the way, appears to be a very popular spot. Too bad we're not Catholic."

"We like it fine here, mom, it's quiet."

"You can say that again. I would go mad here."

"Then it's a good thing you don't live here." Mama shot Nana an accusatory look and they both returned to their own business, Nana to the stove, Mama to her coffee.

That afternoon, they all went for a walk down the road. It had been a long while since Mama and Julia left the house for a walk. Farley danced and twirled in front of them, urging them to continue forward out of the yard, down the driveway and onto the dirt road. Trixie came out of Juanita's yard as they passed and she and Farley touched noses in greeting. He jumped around her and she trotted briskly along with them.

"Joining us today Trixie?" Mama said.

Trixie was Farley's best friend. She was brindle and stout, all muscle, a jaw that could clamp down on bone and never relent. If a neighbor dog tried to mess with Farley, she let them know to mind their own business. Farley was practically Trixie's opposite, long and lean from snout to tail, tan fur with black and white markings. Gangly and meek, he still outran the fastest fox.

Nana looked at Trixie with apprehension. "She's a good dog," Julia assured her while stroking Trixie's big square head. Nana reached out her hand for Trixie to sniff.

In her green rubber boots that looked like frogs, Julia splashed in the mud puddles left over from yesterday's storm. They wandered ahead of Nana. Julia picked flowers and ate them. They tasted like meatloaf and spaghetti. She picked a wild rose and shoved it in her mouth. "Mmmm," she said, "This one tastes like eggs and bacon." Mama laughed. Julia looked up at her and laughed harder. Nana trailed behind in her big straw hat and purple glasses. She looked around, across the field, along the mountain-strewn horizon. Mama stopped in her tracks, "Look, Julia, it's a butterfly." Julia stopped, "Where?"

"Right there, on the rock. Oh, there it goes." Julia caught the sight of the pale indigo wings on a small daisy by the ditch. "Do you think it's a fairy in disguise?" Mama asked.

Julia waited for the fairy to flutter away and then she ate the daisy. It tasted like chocolate cake. She watched her mom greet the neighbor's horse who they had named Poddygrass. Julia looked back at Nana who was content with her own stride.

On the way back from the walk, Trixie was run off the narrow road by an eighteen-wheeler carrying a steamroller chained to its flat bed. When Trixie jumped aside, taking refuge in a near ditch, Mama waved her fist at the speeding truck, "Slow down!"

"Why are there trucks coming down this way? I thought this road ended in the mountains." Nana asked.

"It does or it did. There's an old forest road, just up ahead, and they're putting in a new development on the other side."

"A new development?"

"Yep, just over the ridge."

"Well, that's going to bring so much traffic in here. They'll need to widen this road."

"I'm sure they will, and pave it, and put in traffic lights probably."

"Oh, they won't put in traffic lights. Maybe just a stop sign."

Mama glared at Nana.

"What?" Nana asked.

"All I have is this one little corner of the world. Is there any place left on this god-forsaken planet free of pollution and destruction? People are dying and suffering and we keep consuming and building and bringing children into the world. It makes me sick to my stomach to think about all the suffering and pain."

"That's your problem, Elise, you think too much."

"Well, what should I do, Mom, just block it all out and go about my shopping?"

"We do what we have to, Elise, to get by, to raise our children and take care of our family."

"So, we can screw up our children the way we were screwed up and pass on this legacy of crap." Mama spit a little on the last word and Julia knew that meant it was a bad word, and that she should only repeat it with her dolls and toys.

"Elise!" Nana said aghast before looking at Julia and putting on a smile.

After a couple of days, Nana began to make herself at home. She spent her time outside, sitting in an old Adirondack chair beneath the apple tree, with her big hat and glasses, reading books. Julia looked forward to seeing her there.

Mama tried to keep up appearances of normality. Whenever Nana hung around, Mama busied herself with mundane tasks, but when Nana left the room, Mama slumped down again in her chair. Sometimes, while washing a dish or reading a magazine, her eyes would drift into the middle distance until Julia called her back.

Eventually, Nana tired of hanging around the house and taking walks. Julia heard her tell Mama. "I'm taking her to church."

"What?"

"She needs other kids. You need community."

"I do not. We are fine. Besides, I doubt you're going to find community at that church."

"Little kids need to be around little kids. She's lonely."

"I don't want them putting ideas into her head."

"She's only four."

Mama seemed to consider this before quietly admitting, "I don't like the idea of her leaving the house without me."

"You don't trust me to take care of her?"

Mama turned away as if she were thinking how to answer, but then she drifted and didn't return. She sat in her chair by the window and stared. Nana's face furrowed with concern. "Elise, have you considered maybe seeing a doctor?"

"I've seen doctors. They haven't done anything to help."

"If I had known how bad it had gotten..."

"Please, mother, get off my back. I'm doing the best I can but nothing is ever good enough for you, is it?"

"Elise..."

"Just let me be."

Nana waited a moment before walking away.

The next morning, Nana told Julia they were going to church.

"What's church?" she asked, looking to Mama, but Mama said nothing and Nana responded, "It's a place where people go on Sunday to listen to a man, a priest, talk about big ideas."

Julia wasn't sure that sounded like fun. "What kind of big ideas?"

"Oh, God and Jesus and Heaven."

"But Jesus is a bad word."

"We're Jewish, so we don't really believe in Jesus. We're not really Jewish though either, just our ancestors."

"What's Jewish?" Julia asked. Nana glanced with irritation at Mama and then said, "Never mind. There will be kids there."

Julia jumped up on her toes and cheered. Nana told her to wear her prettiest dress, but not her tutu, and they got in the bright red shiny car and drove to church. Mama rarely left the house. On Mondays, they went to the small convenience store around the corner to stock up on food. Mama said Monday afternoons were best because less people would be on the road. Every few months they drove over the mountain to the big town and spent hours shopping. One time, they brought home Farley. Every time they left the house though, Mama acted strange beforehand, pacing from room to room, mumbling to herself. They couldn't leave without her checking the house over and over again to make sure everything remained in its place, the lights out and the stove turned off. Often, Mama came down with a headache and they had to put the trip off for another week.

Julia liked driving around their village. She saw cowboys on horses and tractors cutting paths across large fields. All the houses were the same shade of brownish orange, like her own, or they were the same elongated metal squares set atop wood and bricks. People in colorful trucks waved when they passed. Julia didn't understand why Mama wanted to avoid people; they were always very nice to her.

The church parking lot was full and they parked across the street. Julia held firmly to Nana's hand as they walked through two layers of heavy doors and into the enormous room, loud with the mumbling of people packed in between rows of benches. At the front of the room, a large stained glass of a beautiful woman like a fairy held out her arms to envelop the parishioners. Julia noticed people bowing and crossing their hearts before entering the rows. She practiced this move in case she needed it later. She heard children's high-pitched voices but could not see them.

When she looked up, a broad tan face with wide smiling teeth looked down at her, hands to knees, "*Mi'jita*! You're here!" Julia smiled to see Juanita. It had been a long while since she visited. "You look so pretty. I love your dress. I wish I knew you were coming. I have a present for you. Who's this?" Juanita and Julia looked up at Nana.

"Hello. My name is Barbara. I'm Julia's grandmother, Elise's mother."

"Oh, how nice to meet you. You must be proud of this one. She's so smart." Nana smiled down at Julia.

"Come sit with me," Juanita grabbed Nana's arm and pulled her to a row in the middle of the church. They squeezed past people's laps. Julia pouted; she forgot to do the bow thing before going down the row. Nana smiled and whispered, "Excuse me," to each person she passed but they ignored her. She sat down beside Juanita who introduced her to the woman on her right, another old lady named Flora. Nana picked up Julia and placed her in her lap. From there, Julia could see to the front of the room. She spotted a couple of other kids, two rows down, sitting quietly in frilly dresses and hoped she would get to play with them.

A man in a black shirt entered, walked to the stage at the front of the room beneath the fairy and everyone grew quiet and listened. The man talked for a long time. Often they would have to stand up, when everyone else did, and kneel, when everyone else did. There were pictures on the walls of a man carrying a log, being whipped and pegged to two sticks. Julia tried to look away but the bloody man hung everywhere. She couldn't rest her eyes without seeing him. She whispered to Nana, "Who's that man hanging?"

"That's Jesus."

No wonder Mama didn't like Jesus, Julia thought, he's scary.

At one point, when Julia thought the man up front would never stop speaking, everyone had to stand and shake hands with the people around them, in front, in back, on either side, and even those people next to those people. Julia lowered her eyes to avoid shaking hands. Juanita shook Nana's hand, Flora shook Nana's hand, but no one else turned to Nana, or even looked at her. She just stood there, looking around her at people for recognition that no one would give. Her face tensed up, her mouth pursed, the way she looked when Mama ignored her.

Afterward, when everyone milled around talking, Nana headed straight out the doors, into the fresh air and open sky. That's when Julia noticed the playground. Already two kids were playing on it. Julia tugged Nana's hand and pointed to the playground, "Please, Nana, can I?"

Reluctantly, Nana set her loose, standing back to watch from the fence. As the church building emptied, more children ran out to play in small packs, the girls kicking off their fancy shoes and the boys taking off their suit jackets. Julia climbed up and over the monkey bars and jumped in the sand. Another girl climbed nearby. Julia asked, "What's your name?" The girl turned away while answering so Julia did not hear her.

Julia played easily with the girl until they climbed up to the tallest slide. The girl went down the slide first, but before Julia could have her turn, the girl turned around and climbed back up the slide. After a couple of times, Julia asked, "Can I go?" but the girl ignored her. Julia insisted this time, "It's my turn," but the girl just turned around and climbed back up the slide until she reached Julia's feet and slid back down again. Julia looked to Nana for help, but she was busy talking with Juanita.

Kids behind her were yelling at her to move and Julia decided to go for it. As soon as the girl reached the bottom of the slide, at the moment just before she turned around again, Julia pushed herself full force down the slide, enjoying the swift movement of letting go, until her legs swiped the girl and they both fell hard to the ground. The girl cried. "Are you okay?" Julia asked the girl, worried. Nana and a woman Julia guessed was the girl's mom were quickly at their sides.

Nana bent down near the girl and her mother, "Is she okay?" she asked. "Did you get hurt?" she asked the girl. The mother ignored her. She took the girl, still crying, by the hand and pulled her away from them. Walking off the playground she mumbled just loud enough for them to hear, "*Gringa salada.*"

"Let's go," Nana demanded.

"But, Nana, I want to stay," Julia whined.

"We're going," Nana insisted.

"No! I don't want to go!" Julia ran and hid behind the slide.

"You come out here right now young lady or I will drag you out of here."

Julia did not move. Nana reached out and grabbed her arm. "Ow," she yelled though it didn't really hurt. She kicked and cried as hard as she could as Nana held her body away from her own to avoid the pelt of little feet and managed to carry her to the car. "I wanted to stay," Julia cried as Nana buckled her into the seat. "I know," Nana said, "but we're not welcome here."

At home, the lights were all out and they found Mama sitting quietly at the table, still staring out the window. Nana shook her head and walked down the dark hall to the guest room, closing the door behind her. Julia held Mama's limp hand, "Mama," she asked, "What's *gringa*?" Mama turned her chin, just slightly. "Foreigner," she said quietly.

"Far'in-er? Why did the woman at the church call us that?"

Mama looked at Julia, "Because we're not from around here."

"Why?"

"Because I moved here to get away from where I'm from."

"Why?"

"Because it changed so much that it doesn't exist anymore. We'll always be foreign, Pumpkin."

"Why?"

"Unlike the people who live here, our family has been moving for generations, trying to get away from someone or something that didn't want us around. Each new place we settled in changed us so that we could never go back to where we came from."

"Why?"

"No more questions, Pumpkin. Let me rest." Mama

turned back to the window. Julia considered the things she said, but they didn't make sense to her. How could a place change so much that it didn't exist? How could people change so much that they couldn't go back? Julia turned on the lights and helped herself to a plum.

The next day, Nana left in the shiny red car before Julia awoke. Julia ran to Mama when she realized the car was gone. "Where's Nana, Mama?" she asked, not expecting an answer. Julia ran outside. She sat in Nana's chair and waited. A squirrel bolted up Tree's trunk. Tree did not look well, its branches were turned down at the ends and its leaves were dusty and dull. Farley was digging for something in the field. He would not stop, even when Julia called him over. A magpie cawed up ahead and she watched it hover on the wind. Julia waved hello to the mountain.

The day crept into evening and Julia began to feel cold and anxious, but she did not move, and no one came looking for her. Farley continued to dig at his hole. Near dark, headlights turned into the driveway and Julia ran to meet them. She hesitated. It was not the shiny red car but a dusty old yellow one. She stood in the headlights, shining on the dark house. The back door to the car flung open and Julia heard voices and then a figure exited and came toward her. The lights pulled away as the car backed out of the driveway. Julia saw Nana and smiled.

"What are you doing outside? You'll get a chill," Nana said.

"Where'd you go, Nana?"

"I had to return my rental car."

"Why?"

"Because I'm staying." Julia hugged Nana's legs. Nana chuckled. "Come on, let's go inside and have something to eat."

# Chapter Five

## Late Summer

Late summer, Tree swayed heavy with fruit. Its apples were large that year, the same variation of half red fading into half yellows and often freckled. The air seemed laden with the scent of sweet juice, even as Tree noticed that the monsoons were fading, a little less rain each afternoon.

No one maintained Tree as they did when it was younger. No hands pruned its limbs, shaping a more lateral growth, or thinned its minor branches to ensure more sunlight reached its fruit. It was no longer irrigated but instead, stretched its complex roots toward the river. Nor was it fed a rich compost each spring and fall. Tree sought nutrients from its own degrading leaves. Still, it thrived as much as the forest aspens.

Tree envied the aspens it saw on the canyon wall, not just because they were wild and secure in their sense of belonging, but because they were never alone, growing in small groves with connected roots, a single organism.

Tree was concerned that its apples were dropping particularly early. It could not rely on Woman and Little Girl to notice. They were foreigners. Tree could hardly imagine the place they might have come from. The local people who lived and worked on this land for generations determined harvest time by the way the winds picked up in the east and the amount of snow accumulating on the mountain tops. Woman used a calendar, a date, to consider such things, a time she read about in a book.

Apples fell to the ground with a thud. Each one letting loose from the branch, springing from Tree with a stinging vibration. Tree watched tiny worms tunnel through the precious pulp that it spent so much energy to grow. Its fruit decayed to a mushy brown flesh, inedible, attracting flies and wasps.

Little Girl approached and Tree could tell from her strut that it was a good day. It stretched a bold breath, not too much, afraid more fruits would slip from its tips. Little Girl went directly for the niche at Tree's base and snuggled into the moist earth. She lifted the turf that covered Tree's largest root and pulled out her tin box. Lifting the lid carefully, she examined each item within as if for the first time. Tree felt the wisp of her curls' frizz against its broad trunk. It leaned in closer to give her a place to rest her back. That's when it noticed the void.

How long had it been there for? Nothing obvious, just a subtle sense of something missing like one might not notice stillness.

Tree shook, trying to replace the missing earth, and its apples fell hard to the ground, raining around Little Girl, immersed in her curious toys. She looked up at Tree, taking notice for the first time. She looked down at the ground, her eyes searching Tree's rotting debris.

Hurriedly then, she shoved her toys back into the tin box, stuffed the box under Tree and ran back to the house yelling, "Mama, Mama, the apples!"

Some time passed before Little Girl returned, Woman in tow, both carrying baskets. "If we waited much longer, we might have missed them. Early this year." Woman and Little Girl began to pick the apples from the lowest branches first, Woman pulling them down so Little Girl could reach. Each time fingers grasped at an apple stem and plucked, Tree felt a slight ping, followed by relief. When all the lower apples were picked, Woman brought her full basket inside and returned with an empty one. Then, she walked around the side of the house and came back with a ladder. She opened the ladder beneath Tree and climbed up it, perching her basket on the ladder's ledge. Woman began to sing a slow song about morning and Little Girl mumbled along with her. First, she picked from one side of Tree and then the other. All the while, Little Girl watched, pointing out any missed fruit. When all the apples were picked, they lifted their heavy baskets and returned to the house, humming.

Tree shook out its branches, swinging a full mane of leaves, unfettered. The lack of weight drew Tree's attention back down to the ground and it seemed that its farthest taproots were floating. Though Tree had a broad system of shallow roots finding nutrients and water, it was still concerned that the empty space below it might be growing. By the next day, the tips of Tree's outermost branches began to drop leaves and dry out. By the end of the week, those branches were dead and breaking off in the heavy winds.

One sunny day, Woman and Little Girl had a picnic beneath Tree. The newest member of the family, Old Woman, joined them. Tree had grown accustomed to Old Woman's presence. She spent hours in Tree's shade, sunk into an old red chair, mostly reading, but sometimes just sitting and listening.

Old Woman took her place in her chair while Woman

spread out a blanket on the grass and put down a basket. They sat and listened to the river rushing, the bluebirds and finches squabbling, the neighbor's dogs barking at a truck rolling down the dirt road. Woman emptied the basket of fresh baked bread, a jelly jar and a hot thermos. When Woman opened the jelly jar, Tree recognized its own scent, the sugary odor of apples cooked down to their purest form. She spread the apple butter onto a piece of bread and handed it to Little Girl who took a long slow bite into her tiny mouth, leaving the residues of her meal on the corners of her smile.

After eating, they sprawled across the blanket looking up into Tree's innermost reaches and made up stories about the shadows that landed on their hands and the clouds that passed above their heads. Tree thought that they did not notice its damaged parts, but later that day, Woman returned, laying a trickling hose at Tree's base, assuming it must be thirsty. Tree appreciated the gesture so much that it did not tell her that she was making things worse, adding to the slow erosion of tenuous earth.

By the end of the month, Tree's roots were weightless up to the thinnest layer of top soil like a child draws the green horizon line at the bottom of a page. Little Girl once drew a picture for Tree. She brought the crayon scribbles right up to Tree and held it above her head for it to see. "It's you," she told Tree. Then she pulled it down closer to her and, still holding it upward to Tree, she said, "Here is your trunk and here is your leaves and here is an apple. Here is Mama, Nana and me." Tree felt glad to be a thing worthy of a portrait, especially the family portrait.

# Chapter Six

## Circus Family

Julia stopped skipping to look around. The leaves had changed, so that patches of gold, orange and brown freckled the canyon walls. The breeze had a hint of a chill. Tree had been limp and dry for weeks already and its harvest came unexpectedly early. Mama tried to water it a bit, but it did not help. Julia worried about Tree. She knew that Mama and Tree were under the same witch's spell and it was getting worse. Mama was feeling it too.

Beyond the apple tree, Nana and Mr. Bob were talking. Mr. Bob was Nana's special friend. That's what Nana called him. After she gave up on meeting people at the church, their neighbor, Juanita, advised Nana to visit the Senior Center. Nana complained for a while about all the old fogies who refused to speak to her in English, but eventually she met Mr. Bob, or Roberto Rodriguez. Mr. Bob was a widower who lived next door to the Senior Center and claimed bingo as his only vice. Julia liked Mr. Bob because he was nice to her and gave her candy.

She had never had candy before the first time Mr. Bob opened his wide palm to reveal the cellophane-wrapped peppermint swirl. When her tongue first met with the concentrated sweetness, she felt an electric jolt singe through her insides and wanted more. She didn't tell Mama about the candy. Mama already did not like Mr. Bob because he was in charge of the development going in on the other side of the canyon wall. "The head honcho," he said with his bellowing laugh. All thought of the development made Mama irate. When given the chance, she always had a protest speech readied for Mr. Bob, including complaints of lost forests, destroyed communities and the offending noise. Nana didn't care what Mama thought of Mr. Bob and he came over most weekends for dinner.

Julia questioned Mr. Bob so constantly about the construction vehicles she saw pass on the road that he offered to take her and Nana to see the future subdivision. With great effort, Julia climbed into the cab of Mr. Bob's big blue truck and sat on Nana's lap. The truck bustled and bumped up the old forest road, newly widened. As they came over the ridge, Julia thought they had landed on another planet. A large chunk of the forest had been cleared away and multiple logs were piled up along the edge. In its place, plots of land were divvied up into perfect little squares. Four houses were in various stages of construction, skeletons of what would someday be someone's home.

Since it was a Saturday, no one was at work, but Mr. Bob took Julia around to see the construction equipment up close. The bulldozer, he told her, cleared the land and made the surfaces, which were once sloped, flat. He explained how the front-end loader scooped up soil and rocks and loaded them onto the back of a dump truck. Mr. Bob let Julia climb the ladder and sit inside the dump truck where she turned the steering wheel back and forth while making grinding noises between her teeth until Nana said it was time to go home. Julia cried when they had to leave, but Mr. Bob gave her a piece of candy and she felt better.

As soon as she got home, Julia ran to Mama, sitting, predictably, at the table. "Mama, Mama, we got to go to the devel'ment and see all the bulldozers and stuff! I got to climb in the dump truck." As the words left her mouth, Julia realized she had said the wrong thing because Mama's eye sockets creased as she gave Nana a look of fierce disapproval. "What were you thinking taking her to the construction site?" Mama said in a low voice, trying to temper her rage. Julia stood beneath them, her eyes searching between their faces. Mr. Bob snuck out of the room.

"I was watching her closely. I didn't let her run around. She loved it. Didn't you Jujubean?" Nana smiled down at her and she nodded her head eagerly.

"I don't want Julia in a dangerous construction zone."

"I understand why you are concerned, but..."

"How can you support this, mom? You know what this subdivision is doing to the forest land, the wildlife, not to mention, what it will do to the community. How can you just act like it's all okay?"

"Maybe the subdivision will be good for this community, create an economy, bring some much-needed amenities."

"But at what cost? The price of living will go up and families who have lived here for generations will be forced to move."

"Or maybe they will choose to move and not be stuck here. Get some money for their land. Make a new start for themselves."

"And lose their culture?"

"The Jewish people have lived in diaspora for thousands of years just fine."

"You don't get it. What about the land?"

"It's not a very big parcel."

"For now, maybe, but that's how it starts."

"Don't forget, Elise, I raised you in the suburbs. It was a great place to raise children. You could run around, ride your bike, visit your friends. It was safe."

"I don't know about *that*."

"Elise, what is this really about?"

"I told you, mom, construction zones are no place for children to be playing."

"Is this about June?"

"You want to talk about that? Now, after thirty years of never mentioning her name, you're ready to talk about what happened?"

"Is that what this is about?"

Mama's eyes shifted as if she were caught off guard and she turned back to the window. "Forget it. It doesn't matter anymore."

"Elise..." Nana placed her hand on Mama's shoulder but she shrugged it off. Nana sighed dramatically and stormed off. Julia branded her brain with the name June, but never spoke it. After that, Mr. Bob and Nana did not mention taking Julia back to the construction site and, though she wanted badly to sit in the dump truck again, she didn't ask to go.

As the sun pushed apart impending rain clouds, Julia noticed snow on the top of her mountain that had not been there yesterday. It looked like powdered sugar. She glanced back at the house. Mama was busy inside, drinking coffee and staring out the window. Mama's quiet time had steadily increased every day since

Nana arrived, as if she had let Nana take over whatever remaining tasks were keeping her awake. Glancing down the hill, she saw Nana and Mr. Bob laughing loudly, caught up in conversation. Farley was still digging at the hole in the field. He had been at it sporadically for weeks. A small pile of dirt piled up beside where he was digging. "Must be a clever critter hiding in there to keep that dog interested for so long," Mr. Bob commented once.

Julia walked into the small wooded area along the eastern edge of their land. Julia was the princess of the forest. Her green gown was camouflaged in the leaves that tugged at her taffeta netting as she traipsed through her kingdom. Conjuring magic was no easy feat. Julia the forest princess had to find just the right words in elfin speak, and just the right melodic chant to catch them in.

She searched the underbrush for a stick. She found one leaning on a nurse log, light and dry enough for casting spells. Swinging it in the air with focused intention, Julia the forest princess said the perfect spell to summon the fairy spirits. Then she closed her eyes and readied herself for the grand finale.

Sure that no one was paying attention, Julia opened her throat and sang with all the sound her little diaphragm could produce, "Just a spoonful of sugar helps the medicine go down..." Mary Poppins was one of three records that Julia owned and played. She loved her red transistor record player, which she could close and carry around the house by its handle. She also had Free to Be You and Me, which was Mama's when she was little, and John Denver's Christmas album, which Mama rescued from the dump. Julia knew all the words to all the songs on all of her albums. "... helps the medicine go down, in the most delightful way." On the last note, she peaked her voice as high as she could stretch it, until she emptied of air. She noticed the pecking sound of a woodpecker under the house rafters before she heard excited clapping coming from beyond the chokecherry trees.

Turning her ear to the applause, Julia followed the sound to a small opening between the trees. Her mouth and eyes opened wide as she lifted her head to behold the huge contraption erected on the Gallegos Ranch. Two giant pipes bent into arches were strapped together where they crossed and staked into the ground. Even more amazing, hanging from the center were two ropes attached to a bar, in which one woman flipped and twisted around like a fancy bird. Beside her, two other women walked on tall sticks like graceful giants, kicking up their stick legs and spinning around. Below them, a man pulled his legs over his head and placed his feet beside his ears on the ground. Julia gasped and ducked back into the trees.

She waved her hands in front of her, jumping up and down, trying to hold in a scream. Amazing, she thought, wonderful, fabulous, all those big words. Peeking again, she noticed this time farther back, near the river, a camp set up with a school bus painted red and green, two small tents, four camping chairs and rocks, circling a pit of ash. Julia turned and ran back to the house. She remembered something about this in a book she had read. She crouched on the floor in front of her bookshelf and began pulling out her picture books one by one until she found the picture of a bunny rabbit flying through the air on a bar, suspended by two ropes. She ran to Mama's side, composed herself and quietly asked, "Mama? Mama?

What's this?" She pointed to the flying bunny.

Mama took her time glancing down at the page and stared at it for a while as if she were looking through it. She answered, "You know what that is, Pumpkin, don't you? A trapeze artist, an acrobat." She began to turn her head back toward the window, but Julia asked again, "And what's this whole thing?"

"You mean, the circus?"

"Yeah, the circus. And what are all the people in the circus called?"

"I don't know. The Circus Family?"

"The Circus Family?"

"I guess so. Why?"

"Because there is a Circus Family living next door."

"Oh really? Does *Señor* Gallegos know about that?"

"I don't know, but they have a trapeze and sticks they walk on and..."

"Stilts."

"What?"

"The sticks they walk on are called stilts."

"Yeah, stilts, and they have a big red bus."

"Wow, Pumpkin, that sounds like a wonderful story."

"No, it's true. Can I invite them to dinner?"

"What do Circus Families like to eat?"

"I don't know," Julia thought about it. Mama just stared as if she had outsmarted her and then Julia answered, "Candy, probably, and cookies."

"And I suppose that's what you want for dinner?" Julia suspected that was a trick question so she did not answer, "Can I invite them Mama?"

"You'll have to ask Nana." Julia sprinted out of the house down the stone path to the apple tree. Farley looked up from his digging and followed after her.

"Nana, Nana!"

"Oh my, what's all this excitement for?"

Julia stopped to catch her breath, "Can I invite the Circus Family to dinner. Pleeeeease, Nana."

"Who's this Circus Family?" Nana asked. Mr. Bob smirked. Julia looked at him, "It's true. There's a Circus Family next door."

"Really?" Mr. Bob said, pretending to take her seriously, "on the old Gallegos Ranch?"

She puffed up her cheeks and pointed, "You can look for yourself."

"Okay, Jujubean, we believe you, invite them to dinner. Now, why don't you go play down by the river?"

Nana didn't have as much time for Julia when she was with Mr. Bob. Julia pretended to head to the river, but when they were no longer paying attention, she veered east and made her way through the brambles back to the Gallegos Ranch. She stayed back and watched the Circus Family practice their dance. The twirling and twisting, bending and spinning of their bodies inspired Julia to try some of their moves. Farley jumped around her, nosing her raised hands. Lost in her dancing, she did not notice that she had been spotted. The man who could twist himself into a pretzel and one of the stilt ladies headed over to her, smiling.

The man was very small and lean and he walked with his shoulders pulled back. His head was shaved and it seemed his smile took up half his face. "Hello," they called out to her before they neared. Julia stood still. She wanted to run but found herself glued to the ground.

The woman on stilts stayed back so she could see

down at Julia. She had short dark hair and a round face with big eyes that were noticeably blue even from a distance. "Are you the singer?" the stilt lady asked.

Julia blushed when she remembered that they had heard her sing. She just nodded. "Well, you have a beautiful voice."

"What's your name?" the bald man asked.

"Julia," she spoke into her chest.

"Julia? That's a pretty name. My name is Sparrow and this is my friend, Sunshine." Sunshine waved.

Julia was delighted that their names fit their appearances. They were creatures, stars and characters, not ordinary people. She wanted to ask them all kinds of questions but did not know where to begin. "How old are you?" Sparrow asked. Julia held up all her fingers on her left hand but her pinky. "Four! Wow, a big girl!"

"Nana says I'm a big girl because I can spell my own name."

"Do you want to come meet our friends?"

Julia nodded and followed them toward the towering contraption, even bigger close up. Farley followed from a distance, unsure about the stilts. The woman on the trapeze slowly lowered herself to the ground. Julia thought she looked like a genie from one of her books. She had hair in a braid down to her butt and tiny blue markings that looked like they were drawn onto her face with a crayon. "This is Gypsy," Sparrow said. "Hello," Gypsy said. "And this is Luna," Sparrow said raising his arm to the dainty woman on stilts beside her. "This is Julia."

"Do you live next door, Julia?" Luna asked.

Julia nodded. "What's this?" she asked pointing to the contraption.

"That's our free-standing traveling trapeze," Gypsy answered.

"What's this?" Julia asked.

"This is a mat in case we fall."

"Do you fall?"

"No," Gypsy smiled.

"Is that your bus?"

"Yep," Sparrow said, "Drove it all the way from Oregon. Do you want to see it?"

Julia nodded. Farley jumped in first and Sparrow helped her up the deep steps. Julia's eyes scanned the interior of the bus. There were bunk beds, a dining table and two benches, a small kitchen and even a wood stove. The curtains were green with big pink flowers on them and there were puppets of all sizes hanging from the walls and peeping out of boxes.

"What do you think?" Sparrow asked.

"It's beautiful."

"Thank you. It's home. Do you live with your mommy and daddy?"

"No, just Mama and Nana." Julia suddenly remembered, "Do you wanna come over for dinner?"

"Tonight?"

"Yeah, Nana and Mama said you could."

"Sure, we'd love to. What time?"

Julia hadn't learned to tell time yet and she forgot to ask Nana what time they ate dinner. "Before it gets dark," she answered.

"Okay."

Julia climbed out of the bus by herself. She sat on her bottom to jump from the last step. She walked back to where Gypsy, Sunshine and Luna were and waved goodbye.

"Bye Julia, nice to meet you."

Julia and Farley pushed their way through the chokecherry branches and headed to the house to tell Mama the news. Mr. Bob sat on the patio drinking a beer and Nana was inside starting dinner.

"They're coming! They're coming!"

"Whose coming?" Nana asked.

"The Circus Family."

"Oh, your little Circus Family, I see," Nana looked over at Mama to share in the joke but Mama was not there, just the empty shell of her body, limp and pulsing, taking up space at the table.

"Their names are Sparrow and Sunshine and Gypsy and, and..."

"What creative names!"

"Yeah, and they live inside a bus..."

"How charming! What do they like to eat?"

Julia realized that she forgot to ask. "I don't know. I can go ask," she started for the door.

"Hold on young lady. Why don't you pick up some of your toys and then you can help me set the table."

"But I don't want to."

"You know the rules Jujubean, pick up your toys or I'll pick them up for you and throw them in the trash." Julia knew that Nana would do it. She did it once before and threw out her favorite dolly, the one that sucked her thumb. She cried for a long time, but Nana would not relent. Before Nana came, Mama never made Julia pick up her toys. Either she let them lay around the house, kicking them out of the way when necessary or she picked them up for Julia while singing a song about sharks in deep waters. Most of the time, Julia helped Mama before she completed the chore herself.

Julia reluctantly started picking her blocks up off the floor but built a zoo instead, complete with lions and giraffes. She did not notice the sky dim until she heard voices outside and then Mr. Bob came in to tell Nana that there were some people there for her. She noticed his voice slow down when he reached the word people.

Julia jumped up, "It's them!"

"Who?"

"The Circus Family!"

"What? I thought you were just pretending."

Julia ran out the door and stopped quietly in front of them. She lowered her eyes and swayed slightly. "Hey there, Julia," Sparrow said with his wide-toothed smile. Julia put her hands behind her back and smiled. Nana followed behind. She looked to Mr. Bob, then Julia, then back at the Circus Family. Eventually, she said, "Welcome, come on in."

"Thank you so much for having us," Luna said. Julia noticed she wasn't much taller than her when she wasn't on stilts. She only had to tilt her head slightly to look up at Luna's shoulder, but turned away quickly when Luna smiled down at her.

"Julia is a doll," Luna said.

"Yeah. Thanks for inviting us," Sunshine said.

"Of course, it's our pleasure. Any friend of Julia's... How rude of me, my name is Barbara. I'm Julia's grandmother, and this is..."

"Roberto Rodriguez," Mr. Bob shook Sparrow's hand.

"Nice to meet you. I'm Sparrow. This is Sunshine, Gypsy and Luna."

"Hello," they said in melodic chorus. Julia beamed to see them in her home.

"Please, sit down," Nana offered them the couch. Mr. Bob sat with them on the recliner, saying nothing. "Can I get you a beer?" Nana asked.

"Thank you, but we don't drink."

"Well, we have water, but I'm afraid not much more. It's so difficult to get anything around here..." Nana's voice trailed off.

"We're fine, thank you," Sparrow answered and the others nodded. Nana returned to her cooking in the kitchen.

"Do you want to see my zoo? I built it."

"Beautiful," Gypsy said. Julia noticed Mr. Bob staring at the blue markings on Gypsy's face and the large wooden holes in her lobes where earrings should be.

"This is a giraffe and this is a lion."

"Very cool."

"Where's your mom?" Sparrow asked.

"She's here. She's having quiet time right now. She probably can't meet you."

"Quiet time?"

"Yeah. That's when she's quiet."

Sparrow chuckled, leaned back into the couch and looked at Mr. Bob. "So," Mr. Bob said, "you guys are camped on the Old Gallegos Ranch?"

"Alberto Gallegos is my grandfather," Gypsy said.

Mr. Bob's face alighted, "Really? Señor Gallegos? How is he?"

"He's good, still ticking. He lives down in Albuquerque with all my aunts and uncles."

"Yes, yes. And so, your parents are..."

"Dolores and Chris Jaramillo."

"Yes, Dolores. She was a sweet girl. And Chris, he was the oldest boy?"

"No, second oldest."

"I remember him. He used to work at the the old lumber mill up in Valle Largo. And your name is..."

"Officially, LouEllen Josefa Jaramillo, but everyone just calls me Gypsy, now. Well, except my family who has yet to catch on."

Mr. Bob let out his big laugh, "Well, people are traditional. I'm sure you know. Not me. I'm all for progress. So, did you grow up here, then?"

"I grew up here until I was ten years old and then we moved to Albuquerque with all my cousins. We'd come up here sometimes to go fishing and camping, but that's it. I went to college in Oregon and studied circus arts and have been there ever since."

"Ah, huh. And, what are you doing here?"

"We needed some place to practice. We're planning on taking our show on the road and we needed somewhere without distractions." Sparrow, Sunshine and Luna all nodded at this. "I remembered this land and asked grandpa if we could stay on it for a while and he said, 'Why not? No one else is using it.' So, that's why we're here."

"Do you ever think about moving back here? You know, coming home?"

"No, not really. This isn't my home anymore. Most people wouldn't even recognize me; they wouldn't want to if they did." Mr. Bob didn't say anything for a while as he considered what she said. Julia decided that Gypsy was *gringa* too. Eventually, Mr. Bob looked up from his drink and spoke, "*Bueno.* Well, welcome back."

"*Gracias.*" Gypsy smiled.

"Dinner is ready," Nana called out from the kitchen, muffled by the sound of an eighteen-wheeler rumbling past the window.

But before anyone could make their way into the next room, a tremor reverberated throughout the house, followed by a sound like a giant straw sucking up the last bits of juice from beneath the ice cubes. From the window, they could see a cloud of dust pass through the otherwise clear sky and everyone, except Mama, ran outside.

They did not have to go farther than the patio to see, at the bottom of the hill, a giant hole the size of their house, like an eraser mark on the earth. Grass and dirt rubbed away to black. Tree stood tall and precarious, just at the precipice of the void. Julia rubbed her eyes and blinked several times. Farley was already beside it, pacing and whining along the edge. Julia remembered that he had been digging in that spot for weeks. "Farley must have digged it," she said to no one in particular.

Mr. Bob led them down the slope. They stared, adjusting their eyes, unsure if they were sharing a hallucination or if the earth had really opened up and slipped away. Nana held an arm out in front of Julia to keep her from nearing the edge. Mr. Bob scratched his head, trying to figure out the mechanical viability of the situation. Luna picked up a rock and threw it into the hole. Everyone waited with held breath for a sound to reverberate back up to them, but they heard only the chirping of birds and the soft autumn breeze through leaves.

Sparrow crawled to the edge, laid flat on his belly and looked down into the abyss. "Nothing," was all he said. Farley whimpered and hid behind Nana. They stood there long enough for the sun to finish setting behind the canyon wall and the harvest moon to rise over the mountain. Nana shook her head, "Okay, everyone, let's go inside and get something to eat. It's dark and there's nothing we can do about it now."

They moved toward inside, feet shuffling, shoulders turned inward. No one spoke as they entered the kitchen. No one spoke as they sat at the table. Mama was there watching the naked branches of the lilac tree out the darkening window be pushed around by the wind, but no one spoke to her. Nana laid food on the table. No one looked up.

"Alright," Nana broke the silence, "Try to eat. You'll feel better."

Over dinner, theories to the origin of the abyss were passed around the table like salt. Luna suggested a meteorite or spaceship. Mr. Bob wondered if they were on a fault line. Gypsy worried that the hole emitted toxins of some sort. Julia thought that it might have been a wizard entrapping a fairy princess in his underground lair, at which Nana murmured, "Persephone." Sparrow shook his head, "I don't know what it is, but it's something bad. I know it in my bones. We need to hold a vigil over whatever is down there."

"Maybe we should contact the authorities?" Nana said.

"Who?" Mr. Bob asked.

"I don't know, anybody, the Governor, the police."

"It's too soon. We should wait a couple days, see if we

can figure out what it is."

Silence and heavy thoughts weighed down on everyone's appetite and they had difficulty eating. Mama sat quietly beside them, her food cold. Sparrow turned to her, "I'm sorry to be so rude with everything going on... My name is Sparrow." He reached out his hand, but she did not respond. Julia tapped her on the arm, "Mama," she said.

"What is it, Pumpkin?"

"I want you to meet my new friends." Mama turned to Sparrow and turned away again. Sparrow looked confused. "Mama's under a witch's evil spell," Julia said.

Sparrow nodded and looked at Nana who was watching Mama with a worried face.

"Thank you so much for the meal," Gypsy said, changing the subject.

"My pleasure," Nana said, shifting her attention away from Mama.

"Um, we were wondering, if it wasn't too much trouble. I mean, we don't want to be in the way, but we were just thinking, if you don't mind..."

"We were wondering if we could camp out on your land," Sparrow interrupted.

"You mean, near the hole?"

"Yes, if we won't be a bother." Nana looked to Mr. Bob and he shrugged his shoulders.

"I guess so. You can keep an eye on it. Just be careful."

The Circus Family helped clear the table, said their goodbyes and walked out the door. Julia watched them make their way into the night, scanning the darkness where the black hole remained imperceptibly beyond.

# Chapter Seven

## The Curse

Julia awoke to the sound of cracking, jangling, rumbling, roaring and Mr. Bob yelling over it. She jumped out of bed and ran outside in her pajamas. Nana stood on the porch drinking tea and watching the giant machine like a dinosaur invade their front yard, crushing the wild yellowed grasses beneath its enormous tread.

"What's that Nana?"

"That's a hydraulic excavator. See that long arm that reaches way out in front of it? And see the long rope hanging from it? There's a heavy hook at the bottom. Mr. Bob is going to lower it into the hole to see how far down it goes."

"Wow."

Nana just nodded, pleased with the ingenuity of Mr. Bob and the great machinery he could conjure. Julia did not want to leave the patio. Her eyes fixated on the excavator, a monster in their midst, towering over the apple tree that towered over her. Her peaceful yard looked like a construction site, just as Mama foretold. Where was Mama? She expected her to come running out, waving an angry fist in the air, screaming at Mr. Bob.

Julia went inside to look for her. She was not at the kitchen table. She went into Mama's room. The shades were still drawn, the light lingered like a dusty shadow— gray and quiet. There were lumps beneath the blanket.

Julia pushed on them and they were firm.

"Mama?" Pulling back the blankets, she found Mama, her eyes open and blank, lying motionless, her breath soft and warm, "Mama?"

"Mama's tired, Pumpkin."

Julia had not known her mother to stay in bed; even in her saddest trance, she still managed to rise and make a show of herself.

"Get up, Mama, get up. You have to come see the hole."

"It's all my fault."

"What are you talking about?"

"I don't feel good, Pumpkin, let me rest."

"But you have to come see. There's a ex'vator in our yard, a big dinosaur ex'vator and they're gonna fish it into the hole."

"Not today, okay? Go find Nana."

Outside, Julia noticed the camp that the Circus Family had set up beside the hole. There were two tents and a small circle of rocks. Nana said she could go see Gypsy and Sparrow, after she ate breakfast and brushed her teeth. She had a difficult time focusing on anything but the clanking of the excavator. It seemed like it took all morning to get it ready. Mr. Bob yelled directions over the roaring engines, but they had not yet entered the hole.

Julia got dressed and ran over to where Sparrow, Gypsy, Luna and Sunshine had a small fire burning in the rock circle. She slowed down to approach them. They were singing—or more like speaking songs—and burning something that smelled like grass and honey. Their eyes were closed so she sat down beside them and waited.

She could see the hole just beyond them. She blinked twice. It seemed unreal to her like a jumbo black magic marker had scribbled something in her yard. She could almost smell the licorice. She thought if she climbed up the excavator's arm and looked down at the hole, it might spell out a word, but she couldn't read anyway. Or maybe it showed a picture of something like a heart or a lucky clover. She looked over at her tree. It looked sad and she wanted to visit it, but she was not allowed that close to the hole by herself. She looked again, the hole seemed closer to the tree than last night. Maybe she imagined it, but maybe it was growing.

The Circus Family's voices were rising and Julia could hear some of the words. She did not understand the big ones. She just sat and waited to be noticed, waiting for the long arm of the excavator to finally descend.

Mr. Bob blew a loud whistle and the Circus Family opened their eyes. "Hi, Julia," Gypsy said.

"What are you doing?"

"We're chanting."

"What's that?"

"It's like praying."

"What's that?"

"Like in church."

"I went to church once with Nana." On cue, Nana appeared.

"Okay, that's the signal. They're going to lower the excavator now," she announced to everyone around the smoldering fire. "That's about ten stories of rope, so when it is no longer taut, we'll know it hit bottom and be able to determine how low the hole goes."

Julia noticed the uneasy gait and compact body of

Juanita, their neighbor, heading down the hill toward them with her dog, Trixie. Farley ran up to greet her and pounced on Trixie who crouched down and barked.

"What's going on here?" Juanita asked, "Are you digging a hole?"

Everyone responded with confused stares, not sure how to explain it.

"Hi, Juanita, so good to see you." Nana and Juanita hugged like old friends. They had become close in the last few weeks and spent many afternoons chatting over tea in the front yard. Julia was glad because she liked her, but Mama did not care for Juanita and her superstitions, so they ignored each other. "I want you to meet our new neighbors. This is Sparrow, Gypsy..."

"I like the pretty designs on your face. Did you draw them?"

Gypsy smiled patiently, "Thank you, no a friend of mine did it."

"Are they there forever?"

"Yes."

"But you're so pretty."

Nana ignored Juanita's comment and continued, "This is Sunshine and Luna."

"Beautiful names."

"They are a circus troupe."

"Like clowns?"

"Kinda," Gypsy answered, "more like acrobats."

"When did you dig this hole?"

"We didn't dig it," Nana said.

"Well, then, how did it get here?"

"We don't know, Juanita, it just appeared last night.

Bob is going to use the excavator to find out how deep it goes."

"Oh no!" Juanita gasped.

"What is it?"

"It's the legend."

"What's the legend?" Sparrow asked. Juanita lowered her small body down on a log near the fire pit and everyone sat beside her, leaning in to hear her story.

"There is an old curse that hangs over this village. My *abuelita* told me about it and her *abuelita* told her. It started a long, long time ago, when the Spanish first came as far as these mountains. They met an old Indian man from the pueblo harvesting mushrooms and asked him the way through the canyon to the north, but he only ignored them. The Spanish men grew angry with him and killed him with a spear to his back.

"A little boy ran out of the bushes where he was hiding and held the old man, crying. He told them with hand motions that his grandfather was deaf. Then, just before he died, the old Indian man opened his lips and said to the boy, 'The earth will grow angry and swallow them.' The old man was, how do you say it? I don't know the English word... *brujo*?" She looked to Nana, but Nana didn't know.

Gypsy answered, "Witch? Shaman?"

"Do you speak Spanish?"

"A little bit. My grandpa is Alberto Gallegos. He owns the land next door. My mother grew up here."

"Who is your mother? Dolores? Oh my goodness, you look just like her. Tell her Juanita Gurule says hello, okay? She's a good lady, your mama."

"Thank you. Please, go on."

"Yes, yes. So, the boy ran away and told the people of the pueblo what had happened and what the *brujo* had said and they passed the story on as a warning. My great-great- grandmother, Maria Rosa, was in love with a pueblo man and he told her the story. They were forbidden to marry so, she had to marry her cousin, Philemon, but she told her daughter the story and now you know it too."

Unwavering eyes stared back at Juanita as if awaiting more answers. Sparrow nodded, while Nana shook it from her head. "Just a fairytale," she said to Julia who looked nervously at the hole and the rope falling lower and lower into it.

Everyone lined up near the edge, waiting for the rope to go slack, a sign that perhaps they had a chance to be saved from the terrible curse. The excavator lurched forward with a disarming grunt and stopped. The rope, still swinging freely in the black void, taunted them with a spin in the lucid emptiness.

Mr. Bob hung his head defeated, then made a motion to the driver to bring the rope back up. He walked slowly around the tree, over the trampled grass, to where everyone awaited him in silence at the fire circle. He spoke, "Well, that's all the rope I've got. What now?"

Nana just stared at him and shook her head. "Let's go inside and get something to eat." Nana clutched Mr. Bob's arm, "Is everyone coming?" Julia and Juanita followed with Gypsy, Sparrow, Luna and Sunshine close behind. Farley and Trixie ran ahead. The excavator driver, Abe, came after to wash up and use the bathroom, finding himself invited to the table for some leftover turkey stew. Everyone sat around thinking about the hole, but not talking about it.

Julia sneaked into Mama's room and left a bowl of soup for her at her bedside. The full bowl remained when she returned in the evening to go to sleep in Mama's bed.

That night, Julia awoke when she felt Mama rise from bed. The room flooded with silver moonlight. Mama slipped on shoes and a robe and headed down the hall. Farley followed. Julia got out of bed with her blanket over her shoulders and crept down the hall behind her. Walking on her little toes, she tried to keep the floor from creaking beneath her. When she saw Mama open the door to go outside, Julia came out from around the corner and followed.

She watched the moonlight gleam off of Mama's shiny hair and the rocks lining the patio. Mama neared the hole. Julia noticed that half of the tree's roots were unearthed and a trickle of the river, diverted, fell into the nothingness. The hole was growing, she was certain. Near the far rim, she could make out the shapes of a couple of bodies in sleeping bags outside of their tents. The void nearing them as they slept.

Mama stopped, her toes precariously dangled over the edge of the hole. She bowed her head, looked in and remembered.

# Chapter Eight

### Best Friends

"Elise? Yoohoo, Elise!"

"Huh?"

"Are you okay? You're so quiet."

Elise's mind had gone blank. She licked her ice cream cone. She had to look at it to remember the flavor. She could only feel the cold against her tongue, but the taste of sweet tang and smooth cream were absent. To keep from thinking about the accident, she imagined a brick weighing down on her chest where all her emotions stirred from. It was strenuous work to sustain a vision, but worth it. Any other thought would be worse. Besides, eventually, she did not have to try anymore. Eventually, the brick pressed her broken heart so thin that it dissipated into the sweat trickling down her back, falling to the pavement below the wood bench where she sat across from her mother, and disappeared into steam. Her heart felt as numb as her cold tongue, her head as empty as steam.

It wasn't so long ago that she had laughed, that they were all together laughing over something that seemed important at the time.

"So, are you going to take the dare or sing the hippo song?" Leah asked. Dare or Hippo was a game that they made up because Truth or Dare was no fun, knowing everything about each other anyway.

"Dare," Elise said. One time, Elise did sing the hippo song when June dared her to eat a gross condiments concoction. She already had an upset stomach. "I'm a hippo, a hungry hungry hippo, I eat up your underwear until I am full. I am fat on panties, yummy yummy panties. See my belly, it's full of poo." Later that day, Elise threw up anyway on her walk home from June's house.

"Okay," June said, "I dare you to call up Andrew and tell him that you love him."

"Fine." Elise picked up the pink phone on Leah's bedside table and dialed his number, which she had written on the back cover of her notebook that one time she had to call him for homework. His mother picked up. "I love you," Elise mumbled quickly into the phone and slammed it down on the base. Then she screamed and covered her reddening face. They laughed and rolled around until June fell off the bed and they laughed even harder. "I have a cramp," Leah strained to say between hysterics, holding her side and curling into a ball. When the laughter finally subsided into short heaves for breath and deep sighs, they quietly stared up at the ceiling.

That morning in school, Leah had broken the news to Elise and June that her family was moving to California at the end of the school year. Her dad got a job. Her parents already sold the house. Elise calculated in her head how much time that gave them together—two months.

Leah's house had a porch that wrapped around it so that you could run out the back door, around the house and back into the front door without ever touching earth. The floors creaked as they walked from one room to the next over the old shag carpeting that smelled like wet dog. It was, what Elise imagined, a farm house would be like, if they lived on a farm. Instead, they lived in the suburbs, near a mini mall that had a kosher deli and a Chinese restaurant.

Half the yard corralled in horses, and Leah rode hers in shows where she dressed in fancy cowgirl outfits and made her horse do tricks. Elise didn't know anything about horses and had never been to one of Leah's shows, but she liked to look at the fancy outfits, all rhinestones and satin fringe.

"I wonder what California is like?" Elise broke the silence.

"It's hot there," June said. She always pretended to know things.

"My dad said we'll live out in the country where there is more room for the horses."

"That's cool," Elise said.

"Sounds boring," June said.

"Yeah," Leah agreed.

"This sucks," Elise said.

They did not speak of it again. In order to forget that it was happening, they continued with life as usual, taking turns going home to each other's houses after school to play Dare or Hippo, riding their bikes to the mini mall to buy a Three Musketeers bar and split it three ways, circling back past Andrew's house in case he might be outside playing basketball. On rainy days, they danced to the Flashdance soundtrack, styled their Barbies and played numerous rounds of Sorry. Until, one day, Leah was leaving.

Elise and June stood outside in the driveway where Leah's family's car was stacked with the last remnants of their belongings. They hung their heads and tried to make themselves invisible as Leah's mom checked off lists and her dad tightened straps. Once the dogs were loaded and Leah's little sister buckled into her car seat, Leah's mom told her to say her goodbyes, it was time to go.

"Bye, Miss June Bear," Leah hugged June, nearly two inches shorter than her.

"Bye, Miss Leah Bean," June handed Leah a letter she had written for her to read in the car. She had cut out pictures from magazines and glued them into the margins.

"Bye, Miss Elly Boo," when Leah reached out to hug Elise, she had a momentary sensation of being a child, and Leah, her mother, comforting her. She did not hug back as much as let herself be hugged. Then she handed Leah a book of quizzes that she made for her to do in the car ride. When she made it, she felt very clever, but as she handed it over, she wished she had made something better, like a poem or a painting.

Leah climbed into the car and waved through the window until she was out of sight. Elise realized that she forgot to tell her that she would miss her. She forgot to take one last whiff of her hair. She forgot to tickle her ribs. She looked at June who kicked around a rock on the pavement. "Come on," she said to her, grabbing her arm, "Let's go back to my house." She did not mention playing Dare or Hippo. They could not play with only two people.

\* \* \*

Mail seemed to take a long time to arrive from California because it took a month before Elise and June received a letter from Leah. Sent to Elise, it was addressed to both of them. Elise and June immediately composed a reply. Then, they placed the stamped letter in the mailbox at the end of Elise's long driveway and waved goodbye to it. Although they waited all summer for a response, they never again heard from Leah. For a while, they wondered if she was too busy getting moved in, then they wondered if she made new friends that she liked better, but, eventually, they just stopped wondering.

By August, it became apparent to Elise and June that no one would be moving into Leah's old house. Instead, as if it had never existed, it was demolished and all evidence of it swept away. June ran over to Elise's house crying and took her to see the site where the house had seemingly disappeared. In its place were bulldozers, excavators and dump trucks sitting idle awaiting the workers to come and start them up. June and Elise stood across the street, holding hands, and stared at the lot. She was gone to them now, like her house was gone.

Over the next few weeks, June and Elise visited the site and watched as construction workers cleared the land for concrete hollows and wooden frames. As they passed, the sound of pounding hammers and buzzing saws replaced the song of birds, filling their surroundings with a sense of urgency. The acre appeared to be divided to provide enough room for four large new houses to go in, each with a small backyard. Where the old maple used to be, a paved driveway ran through the middle of the property and connected all the plots. Two houses were already nearly finished, now surrounded by scaffolding where the workers perched to nail in the siding.

"We should put a curse on those houses," June said, looking straight ahead at the new development.

"What kind of curse?"

"Whoever lives there will forever smell like horse manure."

Elise laughed at this. "And their house will smell like wet dog, even if they don't have a dog," Elise added.

"We should do it for real."

"Do what?"

"Put a curse on the new houses."

"How?"

"Meet me here after dinner."

Elise told Barbara that she was going to ride her bike in the driveway after dinner, but she left the driveway and met June on the corner across the street from Leah's house. June had a bag with her and told Elise to stash her bike in the bushes and follow her across the street. Elise obeyed. June climbed through an empty window hole in the third house, just beginning to be erected, and laid a blanket down on the cold cement ground.

"Are we having a picnic?" Elise joked nervously.

"Just sit down, silly."

June was the one always willing to ring a doorbell and run, even when the people were obviously at home. At school, she put gum on the teacher's chair while her back was turned and was never suspected. She often stole money from her mother's purse to buy candy. June's mom was either really clueless or too busy to care. Although Elise happily ate the candy, part of her felt like an accomplice to June's crime. Instead of feeling a thrill, as Elise imagined June did, she felt worried and guilty.

June pulled out candles, matches and a Ouija board from her bag and placed them with care on the red blanket. Elise looked out of the wooden frame at the dimming August sky. "Wow," Elise said, "You really went all out. Is this some wacky witchy stuff, or what?"

"Shhh," June said lighting the candles and sitting down quietly in front of the Ouija board.

One time, when Elise confided in June and Leah that she wanted to be a wizard, a girl wizard, they laughed at her.

"You can't just become a wizard," June said, "You have to be born one."

"Well, how do you know I wasn't?"

"Because you're not magic, that's how."

"Maybe I am and I just don't know it yet."

"And maybe I am a royal princess adopted by peasants," Leah added.

Elise never mentioned it again to them, but at night in bed, she waited for the clock to turn 10:10 before praying to God to give her magic powers. She didn't want to rule the world or anything, she just wanted to be magic, to talk to fairies and see elves, to play with forest animals and help people. She already felt magic inside of her.

It had been a year since the cat visited her that night. She was terrified at the time. Asleep with her eyes open, body paralyzed, she watched the strange black cat stroll over her and sit delicately on her chest. It looked at her with its bright green eyes and then licked its front paw. Elise used all of her will power to reach out to the cat but as soon as movement returned to her arm, the cat disappeared. She turned on the light and searched the room—under the bed, in the closet, behind the door—but there was no sign of the black cat.

After that, anytime she saw a black cat, she followed it as long as she could, feeling as if it beckoned her. She was sure as anything that it was a sign, a sign from God that she was magic and just like in stories, at some designated age, all her magic would be revealed to her. For the time being though, she had to keep it a secret and continue to patiently pray.

"Now, place your hands here, close your eyes and concentrate." Elise followed June's directions, placing her fingers lightly on the edge of the pointer, eager to get the task over with. June lowered her voice, letting it tremble just enough to sound spooky, "Will you help us to place a curse on this house?"

Suddenly Elise felt her hands jolt and the little plastic arrow beneath their fingertips moved quickly to the upper corner of the board nearest to her right knee. They opened their eyes and looked in the view finder. YES, it read. They looked into each other's eyes, equally surprised. Even though Elise knew that June had pushed it, she still felt a chill under her skin. "Now, take my hands," June said. Holding hands she began to chant, "We curse this house, unwelcome on Leah's land, that all its inhabitants will forever smell of manure and wet dog." Elise giggled at this and June shushed her. "Blessed be. Three times three times three." Then she released Elise's hand and they opened their eyes and smiled.

"Where did you learn that?"

"My sister has a book on witchcraft. I looked up how to do curses but they didn't have it in there so I just read some of the spells and made the rest up."

"Cool," Elise said, relieved that they didn't have to do anything weird like dance naked or lick toads.

"I better get back before my mom notices I'm gone."

"Yeah, me too."

"See you tomorrow?"

"Yeah, 'night, June Bear."

"'Night Elly Boo."

When Elise returned home, Barbara was doing the dishes, listening to a book on tape about a detective who used parrots to solve crimes.

Elise and Barbara lived in a small cottage hidden away in the trees off of the road. No one even realized the house existed until they came over. All the other houses were built close to the road with neatly manicured lawns, but their house, built before the development, used to be owned by an old couple who refused to sell their land to developers. When they died, their children sold it to Elise's parents.

Elise's dad had been gone for as long as she could remember. Barbara said they divorced because they argued all the time and she didn't want to raise Elise in a home with all that yelling. Her father moved overseas for work. He had some kind of job that she didn't understand, involving business and selling things. Every couple of months, he called and she mumbled into the receiver about her grades and friends and then waited through the long silent delay for his response. She spoke slowly, afraid that she might talk over him and miss what he said. He sent postcards from all over the world, which she kept in a cardboard box she covered with stickers and hid under her bed.

Sometimes Elise wished that the house was filled

with yelling, instead of the usual quiet. Barbara worked two jobs and Elise, an only child and a latch-key kid, came home from school and watched television by herself on days when June and Leah were busy. During the week, Barbara edited copy for a company that published textbooks. She commuted over an hour to the city and back and then came home to cook dinner and clean up. On the weekends, she assisted at a home for old people.

"What are your plans for tomorrow, sweetie?" Barbara asked.

"I don't know." Elise said.

"I was wondering if you might want to go to work with me."

One time Elise's mother took her to work with her at the old people's home and she was disgusted by the strange smell of chemicals and decay. Most of the old people wanted her to chat with them. They told her how she looked the same age as their grandchildren or great-grandchildren that they never got to see. She stood politely and answered their questions, until she could sprint from sight to play outside in the courtyard.

"No," Elise said.

"Well, maybe we can do something when I get home from work, like go for ice cream?"

Elise shrugged, "Sure." She went inside her room and shut the door behind her. Elise wondered what June was doing at that moment. June's parents were also divorced, but she got to see her dad every other weekend. He would take her and her sister to the park or the beach or somewhere fun and always let them pick out something to buy.

Elise thought this sounded great, but June swore that

it was horrible. Every time June's dad dropped them off, her mother would get depressed and moody or worse she would pick a fight, saying that he spoiled them. Elise also thought it sounded cool to have a sister, but June claimed it sucked because her sister got all the attention. She figured that June said these things to make her feel better.

The next day, on the way home from the pool, June and Elise were walking past the development where Leah's old house used to be and June said, "Let's go in." It was a Saturday and no one was at work. The construction equipment lingered in a state of rest.

"My suit is all wet. I don't want to go now."

"Come on."

"I'm hungry."

"Come on, don't be a baby, just for a little bit."

Elise didn't want to admit to June that she didn't like being in the construction zone. Since she had seen all the workers wearing hardhats, she assumed that things fell on people's heads. Inside the semi-constructed buildings, she crouched and looked above her for dangling objects.

"Let's play Dare or Hippo," June said. Elise was surprised by this. They hadn't played that game since Leah left. It made her a little sad to think about it. June had been acting strangely all morning. When Elise asked her if anything was wrong, she insisted she felt fine. Yet, Elise could detect a distracted look in her eye like she had when things were uneasy at home and she was about to get into trouble.

"I don't think so, June."

"Come on. Are you a hippo? You hungry for some panties?"

"Shut up. Alright. I'll play."

"Cool." Her eyes scanned the scaffolding that seemed to lean precariously against the side of a house wrapped in foil. "I dare you to climb up there." She pointed to the first level of scaffolding.

"I don't know."

"What's wrong?" June prodded, "Is your belly full of poo?"

Elise did not feel particularly playful. She wanted to get home to go out for ice cream with her mom, but she didn't want to invite June. She decided to play out one dare, then dismiss the whole thing as stupid and go home.

Elise saw a couple rungs of metal on the side of the scaffolding that she could easily reach and climbed up to the first level where she sat and dangled her legs. "Happy?" she said looking down at June.

"Now, you dare me."

"This is dumb."

"Just once."

"Fine. I dare you to climb up there," and she pointed to the second level.

"No problem," June said, kicking off her flip flops. June went up the same route as Elise, but when she got to the second level, she decided to go up to the third.

"Be careful," Elise called from below. On the third story platform, June jumped up and down, testing the sturdiness of the structure. Elise felt the whole thing shake and cringed at the sound of vibrating metal. She held on tightly to the railing in front of where she sat. "Cut it out!" she yelled up to June.

June leaned over the rail and yelled down to her,

"Come up here!"

"I'm fine where I am, thank you."

"God, you are such a scaredy cat. Look it's fine." June leaned over the railing as if she was going to hang from it or maybe do a flip or possibly jump up. But then, the railing broke off or maybe she slipped or maybe she jumped, but she yelled as her body flew past Elise's eyes and landed on the ground below her. Elise stared, frozen. June was not moving. Her left leg was contorted beneath her and her eyes were shut. Softly, Elise spoke, "June?" She tried to yell down to her, but she could not get her voice to raise above a whisper.

Elise trembled as she lowered herself down to the ground, slipping on one of the rungs. She stood over June's body. She waited. She leaned down and shook her, but drew back afraid. Elise turned and ran home, looking over her shoulder the whole time as if someone was chasing her. Barbara was home from work. Elise feared that Barbara already knew, but when she walked in the front door, Barbara lifted her head from the mail and said simply, "Hey, sweetie."

"Hi," Elise answered.

"Are you okay?"

"Yeah, why?"

"You look pale. Do you feel okay?"

"Fine."

"So, you still want to go for ice cream?"

"Yeah."

"Great. Go get dressed."

Elise went into her room and took off her suit. She put on her shorts and tee shirt. Each movement was like someone else was making it and she was only watching from the inside looking out. Someone had taken over her body and she was trapped inside. Someone else sat in the passenger seat of her mother's car, someone else stood in line, someone else ordered ice cream, someone else sat at the bench, someone else licked the drips from around the lip of the cone.

On their way home, she noticed her belly beginning to boil, becoming more rapid until it bubbled out of her. Her skin burned from the inside out. As they neared home, they saw ambulances careening down the street toward the development.

"There must have been an accident," Barbara said, turning into the driveway. The light on the answering machine blinked. Elise hurried into her room. Through the door she could hear the frantic speech of June's mother on the machine followed by a knock. "Elise?" Barbara slowly opened the door. "There's been an accident. June's hurt." For a moment, her internal inferno cooled with relief. Barbara did not use the word, dead. Hurt, meant recoverable. Hurt, required a kiss and a band-aid.

"What happened?" She play-acted. She performed the part of someone concerned.

"We're hoping you know."

"What do you mean?" Her words came out quickly, high-pitched.

"Where did you two go after the pool?"

"We walked home."

"Did you go past the construction site at Leah's old house?"

"Yeah."

"Did you go in?"

"Yeah."

"Did you climb the scaffolding?"

"No."

Elise's mother looked at her for a while with a combination of sympathy and confusion. "When was the last time you saw her?"

Elise remembered June's body, mangled and still, and she began to cry. She fell into Barbara's arms like a baby and let her mother rub her back, shush her, tell her it was all okay, it was all going to be okay, but they both knew that wasn't true.

June was brain dead and in a coma. "A vegetable," Barbara said. Elise wasn't allowed to visit her in the hospital. They thought it would be too upsetting for her. Instead, she rode her bike to the stationary store at the mini-mall, careful not to pass the construction site. She bought June a get well card. When she showed it to Barbara, she said nothing, only looked away. Elise put the card in the cardboard box under her bed.

After being in a coma for three days, June's parents pulled the plug on the machines keeping her alive. The phone rang and when Barbara hung up, she turned to Elise and told her frankly that June died that morning. Elise felt nothing. She only felt the sensation of pretending to feel sad, a mockery of sadness. She wanted badly to act the way someone would act if they were sad, so she lowered her head and did not speak.

No kids were allowed at the funeral. Barbara attended alone. Elise sat on her bed and watched her get dressed in her dark suit and pearls, the smell of her citrus perfume in contrast with the morbid mood. "Why can't I go?" Elise asked.

"They don't want children there, sweetie."

"Why not?"

"I don't know. Maybe they are afraid it would be too upsetting."

"But I'm already upset."

"You won't be forever, Elise."

"Well, how long then?"

"I don't know, but it will probably feel like forever and then one day it won't hurt so bad anymore."

"Then what?"

"What do you mean?"

"Will I just forget that June ever existed?"

"Of course not. Don't be silly. Now, stay here and be good and I'll bring you home a pizza." Barbara kissed her on the forehead and grabbed her purse on the way out the door.

Elise didn't really want to go to the funeral, to stand around and pretend to be sad with everyone. She didn't want people to look at her, to pity her. She felt ashamed to be alive.

Elise later learned that there was a kid at the funeral, Audra Havoway, who she and June always made fun of at the town pool for wearing water wings. Audra represented everything June hated in a girl; she was frail and needy. They called her Cry Baby behind her back. Elise was outraged that Cry Baby was allowed at June's funeral and she was not. Barbara tried to assure Elise that her parents brought her mistakenly, but Elise felt cheated, like she didn't matter.

Once June's body was in the ground, everything returned to a fake sense of normalcy and no one talked about it anymore. Barbara went back to work and Elise stayed home alone during the day. She wrote Leah a letter to tell her that June died. Then, she put the letter in the cardboard box under her bed. She wrote a letter to her future self to remind her to be a better person so that June didn't die for no reason. She wrote another letter, this time to June. She told her she was sorry that she didn't catch her; her arms were too slow and not long enough.

The letters turned into stories. She wrote one story a day. It became a ritual. She would write the story and then, before Barbara returned home from work, she would burn the story under a tree in the backyard and bury the ashes beneath its roots. To make things easier, she stopped writing the stories down at all. Instead, she spoke them out loud, imagining herself pulling them down from outer space and sharing them with her dolls and stuffed animals, the most captive and uncritical audience.

Sitting up in bed, Elise imagined that her room was a quiet cave. She pulled out her stuffed animals one by one from around her pillow and placed them so they encircled her. Then she grabbed the scarves from Teddy's neck and wrapped them, turban-like, around her head.

"Okay, children, gather round," she said with a mysterious tone, "Give me your tickets and have a seat. It is time for the Great Sorceress Elise to carry you far away to a mysterious and brilliant place, called Wonderland. Let me incite a wild tale to alight your fancy. Elise scanned the plastic eyes of each stuffed toy, captive with anticipation.

\*\*\*

*It was not easy for Alice to crawl out of the long dark hole. There were several large roots that assisted with footing, but it was such a long journey with nowhere to stop and rest. When she reached the rim, she pulled herself up and swung her legs over until she lay on her back at the edge of the hole. This place did not look familiar at all, but she was too tired to wonder. Instead, she decided to take a nap. She was soon interrupted by a buzzing that vibrated in her ear like a train rushing through her head. Buzz. Buzz. Buzz.*

*"What is that noise?" Alice said, waking up alarmed, but as soon as she asked the question, the buzzing was gone. She waited for the sound to return until she began thinking about where she might be and the buzzing began again. "What is that noise?" As soon as she asked the question, the buzzing stopped. She waited, perfectly still. When she forgot about the noise and stood to go, the buzzing began again.*

*"Now cut that out" Alice yelled, "and show yourself!"*

*A fly swerved into her face. She swatted it away. "Leave me be, you stupid fly!"*

*The fly must have taken offense to this because it answered, "Buzz. Why do you presume that I am stupid?"*

*"Oh, I'm sorry," Alice said, "I didn't know you could talk."*

*The fly landed on the tip of her nose and she went cross-eyed trying to see it. "Buzz. I am not stupid at all, quite the opposite. I may even be able to help you. Where is it you wish to go?"*

*"Home."*
*"What is home?"*
*"It's where I live, of course."*
*"Are you not living, now?"*
*"I am."*
*"Then, you must be home."*
*"No, no. I sleep at home."*

*"I just saw you asleep by that hole. Buzz. So, that hole must be your home."*

*"No,"* Alice began to wonder if the fly was stupid after all. *"Home is where I spend most of my time and where I wish to return to, now."*

*"Oh, well then,"* said the fly, *"I suspect you want to go this way, follow me. Buzz."* And so, Alice, not having any better ideas, followed the buzzing of the fly as it zipped down the trail through the forest.

When the fly stopped its buzzing, Alice was deep in the center of the dark woods. *"Hello? Fly?"* she called but she heard nothing in response. She was tired and had no idea where she was. Frightened, she sat on a log and cried. Over her sniffles and whimpers, she heard the sound of laughter in the near distance. She jumped up and eagerly followed this welcoming new sound. She came to a clearing in the woods and there in the middle of the sunlit meadow was a young girl, her back to Alice.

From the slope of her shoulders and the honey color and soft curls of her hair, Alice thought it was her sister and called out to the young girl doing something out of sight with her hands, an action that caused her head to bob slightly. *"Sister!"* Alice called out. The girl stopped moving but did not turn around right away, *"Sister, is that you? It's me, Alice."*

The girl slowly revolved and Alice jumped back in fear, for it was not her sister at all, but a china doll with porcelain hands and a porcelain head that blinked and smiled and tilted to the side with curiosity. *"Alice? Is that you? I have been waiting for you all day, knitting you this lovely scarf."* The doll lifted the scarf for Alice to see and it was identical to the scarf that her sister had been making her when she *saw her last. Alice was uncertain how to proceed. This doll certainly thought that it was her sister. Not in her nature to be rude, she decided to play along.*

*"Where is mother, sister?" Alice asked with false calm.*

*"Oh, you don't want to see her. She's very upset that you disappeared."*

*"But I am back now and would very much like to see her."*

*The doll neared Alice, but she stepped back, "Is something wrong, sister?"*

*"Oh no," Alice said trying hard to sound normal, "I just thought, well, I better let mother know I am here."*

*"Very well, then. Just follow the trail through the garden and you will find her there."*

*"Thank you," she said, cautiously skirting the meadow.*

*"You're acting quite strange," the doll said. But Alice took off into a trot as soon as she hit the trail and did not look back.*

*The garden was very big and the plants towered over her. The deeper into the garden she went, the less manicured it became, until she nearly suffocated at the stems of enormous blossoms. She did not know whether to move forward or back. She weighed her options when she heard the buzzing of a fly up ahead and ran to follow it. The buzzing grew louder and louder until she found herself outside a log cabin where a woodsmen was cutting down flower stalks with a chainsaw.*

*Alice stood a safe distance from him and waved her arms in hopes of getting his attention. He looked up, but stared right through her as if she wasn't there. "Father?" she yelled, "Is that you?" It certainly looked like her father, though she had never seen him with a beard before. She waved again, yelling louder. The door to the cabin creaked open.*

*Moving closer to investigate, she saw only darkness within. Closer still she crept until she was nearly inside, unable to make out any shapes or outlines.*

*"Alice? Where have you been?" She heard her mother's voice from far away.*

*"Mother? Is that you?"*

*"I was so worried about you. How dare you disappear like that."*

*"Oh mother, I'm sorry, please, let me explain."*

*Just then, out of the shadows, Alice spotted a horrifying face, not her mother at all, but a green-skinned wart-nosed witch. Alice screamed and the witch's cackle made the cabin shake. Alice turned quickly and ran as fast as she could, through the garden, through the meadow (where the doll yelled to her, "I told you mother was mad!"), and through the forest, all the while looking behind her to see if the witch followed. But that lead to her fatal mistake because as she neared the edge of the forest, she looked back one last time and did not see her right foot step directly into the hole. She gasped before realizing she was falling endlessly back to where she had begun.*

She clapped her hands twice, "The end. Please exit through the side door. Thank you." Elise smiled as she unwrapped the scarves from her head. She felt marvelous, just for a minute.

By September, she reluctantly returned to school. Elise had Ms. Breckenheimer for 6th grade and she sat next to a new girl named Libby who had just moved to town from upstate. Libby taught Elise how to fold her notes into circles and to draw dogs with their tongues hanging out.

On the way home from school one autumn day, Elise spotted a dead cat next to the sidewalk. Its black fur glistened in the grass. The cat looked delicate and beautiful as if it had just laid down and went to sleep and in sleep, it stopped breathing. She heard that could happen to old people. She imagined the cat was old.

She wanted to pick it up and hold it, but Barbara had strictly ordered her not to pick up dead things—they carried germs. Instead, she lay down next to it, not caring about the dirt in her hair or that someone might see her. Through a veil of dampened lashes, she held vigil for the cat—a blue-black blur, a watery abyss.

# Chapter Nine

## Talented

Elise's 6th grade teacher, Mrs. Breckenheimer announced that everyone in her class was required to participate in the school talent show. Elise's heart thumped thick inside her rib cage at the news, sure that her world would implode into a million jagged pieces if she had to stand in front of the whole school and perform. After lunch, she begged Mrs. B to let her out of it.

"I'm sorry, Elise. I know you've had a rough year," this was how adults did not mention June, "but if I make an exception for you then everyone else will expect to get out of it, too. Maybe it will be good for you. What is your special talent?"

Elise shook her head.

"Can you sing?"

"No," she mumbled.

"Dance?"

"No."

"Do you know any magic tricks?"

"No."

"Well, I'm sure you have many talents. Why don't you think about it over the weekend and we'll talk again on Monday."

Elise dragged her feet out to the playground where she sat with her back up against a boulder and watched the other kids tagging each other, hanging off the old metal slide that got too hot in the sun, yelling out, "Safe!" Elise hated the idea of being tagged, the boys always pushed and the girls laughed in a way that embarrassed Elise.

Elise had not made any new friends that year. The other girls seemed disinterested in Elise and she understood that her sulking didn't help. But she didn't want to stop being sad.

She knew that if June and Leah were there, they would get together after school and choreograph a song and dance for the talent show. June would teach them her disjointed movements that she called "avant garde" even though she didn't know what it meant. Leah would carry the tune when June and Elise were off-key.

Elise turned on the television as soon as she got home and lost herself in soap operas. When Barbara returned from work, Elise told her over the usual Friday spaghetti dinner that Mrs. B was making her participate in the talent show.

"That's great, Elise! What are you going to do?"

"No, you don't get it. It's not great, Mom; it's terrible. I don't want to perform in a dumb talent show."

"Why not? You're so talented."

"No, I'm not."

"Of course you are. Why don't you sing? You used to sing all the time before."

Elise knew that Barbara said "before" to encompass all things that happened "before" June's death.

"I hate to sing."

"What? I thought you loved to sing," Barbara said while twisting noodles around her fork.

"Well, you thought wrong." It was clear to Elise that her mother didn't know anything about her.

"Why don't you do a dance?"

"By myself?"

"Why not?"

"In front of everyone?"

"Well, what did Mrs. B say?"

"She said I had to be in the show and that I should think about it and come up with something by Monday."

"Why don't you do something with one of your friends?"

Elise wondered who Barbara was referring to. "Just forget it."

"Okay, Elise, what do you like to do?"

She had never asked Elise a question like that. Elise wanted to reward her with an answer. She tried to think of something. "Tell stories?"

"You like to tell stories? I didn't know that."

"You wouldn't," Elise mumbled under her breath.

"Excuse me?"

"Nothing."

"Well, you can't very well get up there and tell a story. That's not really a talent anyway, is it?"

Elise shrugged, "You asked."

She regretted that she had confided in her at all. Asking to leave the table, she went to her room and muffled her tears in her pillow while Barbara did the dishes and listened to her book on tape. Elise wanted to smash the small boom box that Barbara kept in an alcove above the sink. She listened to her books more than she listened to her own daughter.

Elise should not have been surprised that her mother

took the teacher's side. She had done it before. In the fall, soon after returning to school, Elise wrote a story about June. She wanted to imagine where June went after she died. Since, Barbara was not religious, her answers about the afterlife were always vague. Elise wanted to create her own afterlife for June, so she wrote a story and turned it in to Mrs. B for an assignment.

In the story, June lived on a quiet lake on another planet in another galaxy. She spent her day conjuring up anything she could imagine. Some days she made a field of strawberries appear and other days she imagined a party of princesses to play with her. Elise was very pleased with her story. The day after she turned it in, Mrs. B called her mother in for a conference and they spoke alone in her office while Elise waited outside. She was hoping that Mrs. B was telling her mother what a great storyteller she was, but instead, when they exited the office together, Barbara had a gloomy face on.

At home, Barbara told Elise that she was not to make up any more stories about June or death anymore. When Elise asked why, Barbara said, "They want me to send you to a shrink."

"What's that?"

"It's someone who will tell you that you've got problems and give you a bunch of pills you don't need to solve the problems you don't have."

Elise didn't want to talk to a shrink, so she didn't write another story for Mrs. B again.

Maybe her mother needed a shrink. Barbara had been miserable for as long as Elise could remember.

Elise had a sense that things worsened after her father left, like maybe he took the last bit of hope for happiness that Barbara had. People used to tell Elise that she looked just like her father. She certainly didn't resemble her mother who was dark and big boned. Maybe Barbara saw Elise's father in her and that is why she hated her so much and tried to make her life miserable. Well, it worked.

As the weeks passed, Elise continued with life as usual, head in her books at the back of her class, recess spent watching kids play, afternoons absorbed in soaps. But always in the back of her mind loomed a fear of the talent show. Mrs. B did not ask her again what she would be performing, so she took this to mean that she did not care. The talent show neared and the pressure in her gut became unbearable. One day after dinner, Elise vomited up her tuna casserole.

When Barbara asked Elise what was wrong, she did not know for sure, only that she felt overcome by the sensation of being sat on by an enormous beast. Barbara mentioned that there was something going around at the nursing home where she worked and decided to keep Elise home from school.

Elise loved being home during the week. She sat in front of the television all day long switching the channels from her location on the couch, moving from cartoons to talk shows to soap operas while her brain registered everything and nothing. She did not vomit once. Barbara sent her back to school.

Upon her return, she realized that life had moved on in her absence. Some students were spending their recess period painting sets for the talent show while others practiced their performances. Elise sat in the auditorium and watched.

Four of the girls, including Libby, were choreographing a dance number to a Pointer Sisters' song. Libby, who had just moved to their school district, initially befriended Elise until she became captivated by the force of Amy, Alison and Jessica. Amy and Alison took dance classes together at the mall so they were demonstrating step-ball-changes and heel digs.

Elise imagined that she joined them, copying their movements with her particular brand of clumsiness and they laughed along with her as she stumbled through the pirouette. Amy and Alison became Leah and June. June tried to trip her. Leah copied her awkward footing and then demonstrated the move again with grace. Elise giggled at a funny face June made behind Leah's back. Mrs. B walked by.

"It's nice to see you smiling, Elise."

A fragment of fantasy broke off and landed in Elise's lap as she peered up at Mrs. B. She turned ahead with a sour face and said nothing, hoping Mrs. B would move on, but she just stood there straightening her skirt.

"Are you all ready for the talent show this Friday?"

Elise nodded and did not make eye contact. She was getting better at lying to adults. They only heard what they wanted to hear anyway.

"What will you be doing?" Mrs. B persisted.

"Singing," the word fell out of Elise's mouth and it was too late to shove it back in, though Elise had no intention of singing.

"Oh, how wonderful! What are you singing?"

"Never," Elise spurted.

"Oh? I haven't heard of that song. Is it a new one? I know you kids love that pop music."

"Yes."

"Will your parents be attending the show?"

Elise was annoyed that Mrs. B did not know about her absent father. Shouldn't teachers know these things, be sensitive to them?

"No," she said, "my mother has to work." Of course, this was another lie. In truth, Elise did not bring home the flier about the talent show and her mother seemed to have forgotten that Elise ever mentioned it.

"Well, I'm sorry. Mr. Weintraub offered to video tape it so maybe your mom can get a copy from him."

"Yeah, maybe."

Maybe not, thought Elise, maybe there would be nothing to see. Up until this point, Elise had not considered what she was going to do, but she realized she would need to make a plan. Her best idea was to simply stay home on Friday and if Mrs. B called, she would say she forgot all about it. Her plan was ruined when Barbara returned home from work that day.

"How come you didn't tell me that the talent show was this Friday?"

"I didn't? How did you find out?"

"I bumped into Amy's mom at the grocery store."

"Oops."

"What do you mean by that?"

"I mean, I don't want to be in the stupid talent show."

"Why not?"

"Because, I told you, I don't have a talent and I don't want to get up in front of people," Elise threw the remote control she held in her hand across the room. Her own actions surprised her. She heard it break apart and wanted to go to it, to pick it up and put it back together, but her anger kept her bound to the couch.

"I'm getting sick and tired of this bad attitude. I know things have been rough for you." By "things," she meant losing both her best friends in one summer, "but that is no excuse to stop participating in life. You need to just get up off your butt and get back in the game."

"Fuck the game!" Elise shouted. She wanted to cover her mouth, but could not allow Barbara to see her back down.

"You listen to me, young lady. I don't want to ever hear you talk like that to me again. You will do that talent show if I have to drag you to it."

"No," Elise yelled but it sounded more like a plea.

"Oh yes, and you have lost all your television privileges for the weekend."

"This is bullshit."

"Go to your room right now. I don't want to see your face again until tomorrow"

Elise slammed the door behind her. She threw her pillows at the walls and threw herself onto her bed in tears. She wanted to vomit, but she was empty. She felt completely empty. She deserved this, she thought, she deserved all this pain because she was alive and June was dead and now nothing could be right again.

On the evening of the talent show, Barbara did just as she had threatened and dragged Elise there. She even made her wear a dress lest she lose TV for a whole week. Elise pouted in the car, her arms crossed over her chest. As she stared out the window, she imagined all the ways she could get revenge on her mother.

1) Before the show, Elise would slip away and steal Barbara's credit card out of her purse. She would use it to buy a one-way plane ticket to England to go live with

her father. Barbara would be so freaked out and worried about her. She would be furious to learn she betrayed her for her father. That would teach her not to push Elise around. However, Elise knew her plan had flaws. For example, she did not know where her father lived or if he would take her and she was afraid to fly on a plane alone.

2) Elise would wait until they got back home after the show and swallow a bunch of sleeping pills like that girl did on the Facts of Life. When Barbara found her cold, stiff body the next day, she would cry and swear, wishing she had listened to Elise instead of forcing her to do the talent show.

Both options required too much energy to enact and did not solve the problem of having to perform in the talent show. So she decided to go with option three: humiliation.

When they arrived at the school, Elise said nothing to her mother and scurried back stage with the other students busy primping and practicing. Amy, Alison, Jessica and Libby had on matching pink leotards and striped tights. Elise looked at her own dress, the purple one she loved last year but seemed old now.

Mrs. B looked surprised to see Elise there, as if she didn't expect her to show. "Well, hello, Elise. You look lovely. Are you all set?"

Elise nodded slightly.

"Good. You're third. After the girls do their dance."

"Great," Elise said with concealed sarcasm.

From between the side curtains, Elise watched Amy, Alison, Jessica and Libby performing their dance that she had witnessed so many times in rehearsal. Jessica and Libby were in the back row, just a few seconds behind

Amy and Alison in the front. Still, Elise thought they did a pretty good job. Their parents stood first and the rest of the crowd joined the ovation out of social obligation.

When everyone was seated, Mrs. B pushed Elise onto the stage and urged her from the sidelines to approach the microphone. The lights were hot and shining in her eyes. She squinted into the awaiting audience searching for Barbara in the crowd. She saw a hand in the far left middle row wave to her. Elise had told Mrs. B that she sang a capella, mainly because she had made up the song title and also because she did not expect to be there. So, no music cued up. Mrs. B whispered loudly from backstage, prompting her to start, but Elise just stood there, the crowd mumbling and restless in their seats. When Elise felt that Mrs. B could not wait for her any longer and might come to drag her off of the stage, she turned her back to the audience, lifted the back of the skirt of her purple dress and promptly bent forward exposing her pink and black polka-dot undies to the parents of her peers. She heard the shocked gasp of the crowd and walked off.

The first faces she saw upon leaving the stage were Amy and Alison; they pulled back their chins, glaring at her with a mixture of pity and disgust. Then, she saw Mrs. B, "I'm disappointed in you, Elise. We will discuss this on Monday," she said while ushering a red faced Aaron Kim on stage to play his oboe. Beyond her, a couple of boys from her class gave her high fives and said, "That was awesome!" But, Elise didn't feel awesome. Instead, she felt embarrassed and more alone than ever.

After the show, she waited until everyone left before going to see her mother. Elise hung her head and shuffled her feet. Barbara just turned from her and walked out the door. Elise followed. They did not speak on the way home. Elise went straight to her room and fell into a heavy sleep.

She awoke from a terrible dream that she could not remember. All that remained was an ominous sense of uncertainty. The house was empty. Barbara had left for work at the old people's home. She had given up on inviting Elise to come along. Elise wished her mother was there to steady her from her dream.

Leaving her room, she stationed herself on the couch in front of the television even though it was prohibited. There was no school, no Mrs. B, no Barbara, just the cartoons and court room dramas, family movies and sitcoms. She only stood up to use the bathroom and to get snacks from the refrigerator. Without realizing it, she gobbled down a bag of chips. She followed it with a glass of milk. When Elise heard the sound of Barbara's car rolling into the driveway, she quickly turned off the TV and jumped into bed.

Barbara did not come in to check on her, nor did she call her for dinner. Elise could smell the chicken frying in oil and began to salivate. She entered the kitchen slowly, sleepy-eyed pretending she had only then awoken. Barbara was eating at the table. She did not look up from the paper to acknowledge Elise.

"Smells good," she said. No answer. Elise helped herself to a plate of spaghetti and sat down at the table with Barbara who continued to ignore her. Elise knew that her mother could go on for days like this and it would only work to Elise's disadvantage. A couple of months earlier, Elise stole a ten dollar bill out of her mother's wallet. When Barbara asked her about it, she lied. Barbara searched her room while she was at school and found it in her box beneath her bed. Elise felt outraged at the clear disregard for her privacy, but Barbara did not budge from her silent treatment, even as Elise yelled and screamed with impassioned arguments and denials. Barbara acted like Elise was a ghost roaming the house, moaning her disapproval. Finally, Elise gave in and apologized. Only then did Barbara speak to her again.

Elise understood what she had to do to avoid another drawn-out grudge. "Mom," she said quietly as if she was speaking to herself, "I'm sorry for what I did at the talent show, but I tried to tell you…"

"An apology does not count if it is followed by the word 'but.'"

"I'm sorry, but…"

"Elise."

"I know. I just want you to hear me out. I told you that I did not want to be in that talent show. I don't want to sing or dance or do magic tricks like some kind of monkey."

"What do you want to do Elise? Go tell your silly stories? Is that what you want to do? Do you want to be a social outcast all your life? Huh? Because you're half way there, Elise. I swear."

Barbara threw her dishes into the sink followed by the sound of crashing ceramic. "Shit!" she yelled. She leaned over the sink with her eyes closed taking long breaths. Elise stood near her mother, unsure what to do. She was sick of this whole year. She wished she could take back all the events leading up to this moment, return to a time when she could still feel light.

Elise understood clearly what Barbara meant. She wasn't good enough the way she was. She needed to be more like someone else if she wanted Barbara to be happy. Elise had to decide in that moment who she was going to be.

She used all her strength to unglue her heavy arms from her side and reached out to touch her mother's arm. Barbara wiped her tears with her sleeves and turned to Elise, "I'm sorry."

In Barbara's embrace, Elise allowed herself to let go, just for a moment, of whatever uncommon strength she had been using to hold herself up. But, later that evening, after they stayed up to watch Saturday Night Live together, laughing at the Church Lady's crazy antics, Elise lay awake in bed staring at the glow-in-the-dark stars on her ceiling and realized that she had made a decision. She would have to hide herself away for the time being, in hopes of later recovering what was lost.

# Chapter Ten

## THE FALL

On the first chilly night of the season, when a crystal sheet formed on the grass, Tree felt Little Girl's tin box of toys slip away. Even as Tree squeezed its strongest roots together to grasp at the treasure left in its care, the emptiness stole it away. Tree let go then; there was nothing left to hold onto.

Tree thought of Mountain, the one that stood over it all its life, the only one it knew. But all mountains were the same anyway, all one and the same. The winds told it that.

Tree thought of Woman. Once, while Little Girl napped in the sun, Woman got up close to Tree, lining up her torso against its trunk and wrapped her skinny arms around it, her hands meeting on the other side. She looked up into its angular branches and took a deep breath. Tree could feel the weight of her body like an anchor entrenched in rock. Then, she spoke to Tree for the first and last time.

"We are the same, you and me."

She waited as if Tree might answer. Instead, it could only try to absorb her dimming light, her rapidly shrinking force and instill her with a lighter one, just for a while. Not much, but for a moment, part of an embrace, something it never hoped to ask for.

She slumped down on the ground at Tree's base, her

spine curved in like a cocoon. Tree wanted to show her the butterflies, but she got up and walked away. Tree wanted to show her how time changes things, the way its leaves grew back into golden buds and white blossoms in the spring, but she was already gone.

Tree thought of Little Girl and remembered those times when she was most still, back up against its bark, breathing light as a flower. Light like flowers. The breathing light of flowers.

Memories slipped away. Faces and words disappeared. Everything falling away like fresh ash to the atmosphere.

Tree slipped into the hole at dawn when the sky turned periwinkle blue and the sun had not yet emerged. No one was there to see it take one last breath and disappear.

# Chapter Eleven

## WAKE UP

On the third day of the hole's appearance, Tree was swallowed up and disappeared. Julia wailed as if her fingers had been closed in a door jamb. Nana held her close and tried to soothe her, but she continued to cry. Sparrow put his leg behind his head and hopped up and down, but this only made her cry louder.

The hole had begun to creep up the hillside, taking the field of wildflowers with it. The house was sure to disappear next. That same morning, the river flowed into the hole. Mr. Bob and Abe used the excavator to divert the river around the rim. They wanted to keep people in town from investigating. Abe said that if word got out about the curse, people would show up in droves with all their cousins and try to convince the priest to do an exorcism. Julia began to think that maybe these adults didn't know everything after all. They were pretending that there wasn't a problem when it was obvious to her that there certainly was one. The thought made her cry even harder.

"What's with all this crying?" came a voice from the doorway. Julia looked up and stopped. They whipped around to see Mama standing on the patio in Julia's favorite dress, the red one with pink and yellow flowers. "What's with all this doom and gloom on such a beautiful day?" All eyes watched her wander to the flower beds along the front of the house. Inhaling deeply from her choice of sunflowers and Mexican hats, she did not notice the stares. She hummed softly under her breath causing some to tilt their ear.

Julia jumped out of Nana's arms and ran to Mama. "Hey, Pumpkin. How is my beautiful girl?" Mama leaned down and gave her a hug. Julia held on tight, afraid if she let go Mama might disappear. But she was not given that option, "Go inside and get a vase of water for my flowers, please." Julia rushed inside and grabbed the ceramic vase on the buffet table. She stood up on her stool and turned on the water, filling the vase halfway as Mama had taught her. She shuffled back outside, meditating on keeping the vase rim dry.

Mama shook hands with the Circus Family as if meeting them for the first time, as if she hadn't already had dinner with them, or they hadn't been camping in her yard for the last two nights. They smiled, eagerly captivated by her unusual mood. Nana stood behind them, looking on wearily.

"Here you go, Mama," Julia handed her the vase.

Mama put her fresh picked stems in the vase and placed them on the wobbly picnic table. "There, that looks lovely. Don't you think so, Bob?" That was the first time Mama had spoken to Mr. Bob when it wasn't completely necessary.

"Beautiful, Elise. Lovely," Mr. Bob answered.

"What is the plan for today? I thought we could go for a walk in the forest. It is such a beautiful day. Julia can sing some of her songs for us along the way. What do you think?" Her eyes met with the faces around her. Gypsy and Sunshine looked at each other and back to her, nodding. She led the Circus Family out of the driveway and down the road toward the forest. Julia and Farley ran ahead. Mr. Bob and Abe followed, smiling and gesturing, "It is a beautiful day," "The sun feels good," "No rain." Nana trailed behind last, looking over her shoulder back at the hole.

Along the way they passed Juanita's house. She was just on her way over with some fresh apricot *empanadas*. "Juanita!" Mama hollered. "We are going on a walk to the forest. Come along with us, won't you?" Juanita looked at Nana who shrugged and then back at Mama.

"Okay, why not? I could use a walk."

Trixie took her time, steady speed ahead, and Farley jumped on her rear, propelling her on, excited to be going for an adventure. Julia took Mama's hand and Mama looked down at her, smiling. Her hand was warm and dry. When she moved her head just right, the sun shone around her like a golden crown.

Julia glanced back at the crowd following behind, inspiring her to improvise a song about flowers, friends and forests.

When they entered the forest, they meandered along the river trail until they reached the meadow where Mama and Julia used to picnic. "Let's rest here in the grass. We can have some of Juanita's *empanadas*," Mama said, folding her dress under her as she bent her knees down to the ground. Everyone squatted in a circle like children and Juanita opened up the foil to release the fresh scent of warm baked wheat and sweet fruit. She passed it around.

"Tell us a story, Mama," Julia asked.

"Oh, no. No one wants to hear a story." The group

mumbled and nodded in response, filling their mouths and tearing off portions of *empanada*. "Okay, then." When Mama began, her eyes widened in her head, scrunching up her forehead against her crown. She opened up her arms to invite the tale in and searched each captivated face.

*The forest suddenly grew dark and Tree sensed it was being followed. A shadow lurked just out of sight. Tree hurried its pace, nearing the edge of the forest. Once in the open field, Tree relaxed, lowering its tired limbs.*

*At the other end of the field was a house and outside of the house, there was a girl jumping rope. Tree glanced behind it once more before proceeding. The girl was singing a song, its rhythm in time with the rope whipping against the dirt. Tree watched from a distance. When the song ended, the girl turned and spotted Tree. She looked at it curiously and then asked, "Hello?"*

*"Hello," Tree answered. The girl stared at Tree and Tree became self-conscious. It ran its leaves along its trunk, straightening its stratified bark.*

*"Where did you come from?" the girl asked.*

*"From the forest."*

*"But you are an apple tree; you don't belong in the forest."*

*"I was taking a walk," Tree said. The girl nodded.*

*"Was it a good walk?" she asked.*

*"It might have been, except that I think someone was following me."*

*The girl nodded again, "That may be so. A witch lives in those woods. My mother told me not to go in there or the witch will steal me away."*

*Tree tried to stifle a chuckle.*

*"What's so funny?"*

*"There is no such thing as witches."*

*"Of course there is. What was following you?"*

*Tree thought about this for a while. It knew for sure it was not an animal because the stalker made no sound upon the ground as if it floated. "Perhaps it was a ghost," Tree replied.*

*The girl laughed, "You believe in ghosts but not witches?"*

*Tree was unsure what it believed. The girl invited Tree to play a game of jax. Bouncing the small ball was easy enough, but picking up the jax proved too difficult. Tree did its best, leaves fumbling over the small metal pieces.*

*A woman walked outside and told them that it was time for lunch. "This is my new friend," the girl said. Tree wiggled up straight and tall in order to better present itself. The woman looked Tree up and down.*

*"Well, you better come in for lunch then," the woman said.*

*Tree and the girl stopped their game and ran inside. The house smelled of freshly baked bread.*

*"Wash your hands," the woman said.*

*At the sink, Tree ran its leaves under the water until they glistened and scrubbed its bark with a brush. Tree sat at the table and the woman handed it a sandwich. "Thank you," Tree said. The woman smiled. Tree ate slowly, savoring each bite of sticky nut butter and tart jelly wrapped in crispy bread. Tree had not realized how hungry it was until it began to eat.*

*The walk through the woods was much longer than it had anticipated and now it could not remember anything about its home. It remembered leaving a large orchard in the dark of night while the other trees slumbered. Was it running away? From something or to something? Tree could not revive its memory and decided it wasn't important. Maybe it could live there with the girl and her mother?*

*A thunderous dissonance rose up from outside and filled the house. They turned their heads toward the door. The woman cautiously stepped outside. Tree and the girl followed. In the middle of the meadow hovered a dark and shifting form, difficult to focus on. Within the murky cloud was a face, gnarled and green, connected by sinew to a crooked torso and hands curled like claws.*

*"It's the forest witch," said the woman.*

*The girl looked at tree and said, "I told you so." Tree realized she was right, the witch was the one following it in the woods.*

*"What business do you have here?" the woman called out to the witch.*

*"Give me the tree and I will not harm you and the girl."*

*The woman looked at Tree, examining it from roots to fruits, trying to determine its worth. "What do you want with this tree?"*

*"Not that it is your business," said the witch, "but I want its heart."*

*Tree gasped and brought its branches tight against its trunk, guarding its heart.*

*"You can't let her take its heart," the girl pleaded, but the woman did not look as certain.*

*Tree searched for an escape, but it knew it could not move fast enough to get away. It looked at the worried faces of the woman and the girl and said, "I will go to her. I do not want to cause you any harm."*

*As Tree walked slowly out the door, the girl cried. The*

*woman held the girl close to her, covering her eyes. With each step closer to the witch, Tree shivered and its apples fell with thuds around it. Up close, the old hag shifted in and out of the haze like a reflection in water. Tree did not look too closely for her eyes were red and entrancing.*

*The murky fog began to rumble and roar and Tree shut its eyes tight. The girl could not bear to wait for the worst. She had no fears to hold her back. She pulled out of her mother's arms and ran to Tree. Tree felt little hands grasping at its trunk. It looked down and the girl was there beside it. The woman was running close behind "Come back," she yelled. She turned her body toward the witch's whirlwind to shield the girl who crouched low to the ground at Tree's roots. The wind was tossing her hair around in all directions at once, and she could barely see through it.*

*"No matter," was all the witch said before she sent streams of black smoke trails through the woman, over the girl's head and into Tree where they grabbed like hands at its beating heart and tore it out. The woman collapsed and Tree turned to wood. Its roots sank deep into the ground, grabbed hold of the boulders below, and stiffened.*

*The witch cackled and pulled the heart into her mist, which swirled about like a tornado until she took a form, a woman that might have been beautiful except for the red of her eyes. She spun around one more time and disappeared.*

*The girl sat up and cried over her mother. Tree could not move to hold her, could not speak to comfort her.*

*The woman soon awoke, disoriented, remembering nothing of what happened. Her mood was never quite the same after that, drifting sometimes in and out of a dark fog. Only the little girl remembered what Tree used to be, only the little girl understood Tree's fate.*

\* \* \*

Gypsy spoke first, "That was a wonderful story, Elise."

"*Maravilloso!*" Juanita added, "I didn't know you told stories. My sister used to tell me stories all the time when I was a little girl. I just loved them."

"Elise has always been a talented storyteller," Nana said. Julia noticed Mama squirm, as if her side hurt.

"Let's head back to the house," Mama said and stood up, brushing the leaves from the back of her dress. Julia held Mama's hand the whole way home.

Entering the yard, Julia avoided looking at the hole, eyes fixed on the door. She thought she could hear the sound of earth crumbling, rocks stumbling and falling before they disappeared. She feared to see how close it had come to the house, if it had noticeably neared.

Inside, everyone gathered instinctively around the table while Nana cooked up chocolate banana pancakes. They gabbed about insignificant things like high school basketball games, the neighbor's loose cows, and weather.

Abe spoke. Everyone listened because he hardly ever said a word. Abe had a comfortable demeanor that spoke for him. "We stopped work on the development today."

"Really, why?" Nana asked Abe, although she looked at Mr. Bob, who nodded.

"The pueblo is protesting. A bunch of elders went down there this morning and blocked the bulldozers, so Bob told us to stop work until things got resolved." Julia imagined the pueblo elders. She had never seen real live Indians before, only photos in Mama's old National Geographic magazines that she kept piled high in the laundry room for collages. Julia couldn't remember the last time they did a collage or any art project together.

She and Mama used to paint together all the time. Mama would paint a portrait of Julia or some fruit or the sky while Julia piled colors onto the page until a mud puddle formed. Mama always loved her mud puddles and posted them on the fridge door.

Mama wavered between calling them Indians and Native Americans so Julia just called them dancers because they were always dancing in the photos. Large crowns of feathers grew up out of their heads the way turkeys looked when they puffed up big. Heads down, knees high, they danced with magic wands or rattles, veering in a tight circle toward the center. They were robed in beaded dresses and Julia wished she was an Indian. This is how she imagined them dancing in front of bulldozers.

"Bob, why didn't you say anything?" Nana asked, surprised.

Julia looked around at everyone staring intently at Mr. Bob who hunched over his food. He finished chewing and spoke, "Someone leaked word to the pueblo tribal government that artifacts were found on the site—arrowheads, pottery and such. They are going to the county commissioner today to try to get the developer's permit revoked." Julia saw Mr. Bob and Abe lock eyes in conspiracy. Nana must have noticed too because she said, "I wouldn't suppose you had anything to do with this?"

"Of course not," Mr. Bob said, keeping his eyes cast down.

"Well, I think that's wonderful," Mama's voice picked up the silent tail, "I hope they cancel the whole thing, no offense, Bob, but I have never held my tongue when it came to my opinion on that development and I think it's just plain obnoxious." Everyone laughed at this, which Julia thought was strange, but she laughed too, even louder.

"Me too," Juanita said and they smiled at each other. Julia was so happy that they were getting along. "Me, three," Gypsy said.

"Maybe things will be better now," said Sparrow, "I mean, with the curse and all." No one responded, their eyes lowered onto their syrup-drenched plates.

Julia wondered if everyone was thinking of the hole, like she was. She missed Tree. She hoped that Tree would come back.

After lunch, Mama took Julia into her room. Mama's room always smelt like honey and cedar chips. Everything was warm in there, even in the winter when the window fogged up with icy condensation. Mama lit the candle on a gold stand beside her painting of apples. "I want to give you something." Julia loved gifts. "This necklace belonged to your daddy's mother and he gave it to me when we first got married." From the thin gold chain, hung a gold heart. Julia held it with both hands like she did with something fragile. Mama knelt down beside her. "You know I love you, right, Pumpkin? You know I'll always love you and always be with you, right here." Mama pointed to Julia's chest where the little bones caged in her heart.

"I know, Mama. I love you, too." She wrapped her arms around Mama's neck and felt her heart full of lightness.

When Mama pulled away, she wiped under her eyes with the cuff of her cardigan. "It's a locket, look," Mama opened it up and inside were two brown faded photos, a man on one side and a woman on the other. The man had a funny mustache and wire glasses and the woman wore her hair in a bun at the top of her head, her dress neckline all the way up to her chin.

"They're funny," said Julia laughing with resonant glee from receiving such a precious gift.

"That is your great-great-grandmother and this is your great-great-grandfather." She pointed at the tiny faces with the tip of her pinky.

"Can I meet them?"

"Oh no," Mama chuckled, "They're long gone. It's just a family heirloom."

"What's an heirloom?"

"Something passed down from parents to children."

"Where's Daddy, Mama?"

"I don't know, Pumpkin."

"Mama, why did you leave Daddy?" Julia had always assumed that Mama left Daddy and not the other way around, and Mama never discounted this theory.

"Because, I guess, I didn't want to infect him."

"What does 'infect' mean?"

"Like when you have a cold and you sneeze on someone and they get your cold too."

"Are you sick?"

"In a way."

"I miss him."

"Do you remember him?"

"No."

Mama turned her face away. "I miss him too. You'll see him soon, promise." This idea pleased Julia. Mama never spoke of Daddy before, so Julia felt certain that she did not make this promise lightly. Julia imagined Daddy there with all of them, the perfect addition to an already wonderful day.

She practiced opening and closing the locket. "Be careful with it. It is very fragile. You're probably too young for something so important, but I wanted to make sure you got it," Mama said. She rummaged through her drawers and then her closets, dark fabrics covered in flowers slipped through her hands. "Here it is!" She pulled out a green silk robe with small golden cranes embroidered around the hem.

"What's that Mama?"

"This is a kimono, a Japanese robe. I've had it for so long I don't remember where I got it from. I never wear it. I thought it would be perfect for Juanita. I can see her wearing it in her garden. Wouldn't that be a silly sight?" Julia nodded her head and giggled, "That's silly." She handled the locket. "Do you want to put that on?" Mama strung the necklace around Julia's neck and fiddled with the clasp. "There. Let me see." She covered her mouth with her long fingers and stepped back, "Beautiful. What do you say?"

"Thank you, Mama." Julia followed Mama into the living room where everyone sat around drinking coffee. The room smelled of roasted chocolate.

"Juanita, would you be interested in this robe? I thought it would look lovely on you." Mama held the robe up casually.

"Oh, *que bonita*! You don't want to give that away, do you?" Juanita exclaimed. She reached out and rubbed the fabric between her fingers. "I like it. So pretty."

"Put it on. Let us see," Mama insisted. Juanita struggled to get the kimono over her shoulders. It did not fully close around her but she held it together and spun around. Luna, Gypsy and Sunshine oohed and awed. The men clapped.

"I never wear that old thing anymore. I want you to have it. Consider it an apology gift."

"You don't have to do that."

"I want to."

"Well, thank you so much. I love it." Juanita reached out her arms and Mama bent close to receive her hug. Julia figured it was dress-up time and went to her room and got a princess dress to model for everyone. More clapping followed.

"Elise, can I talk to you for a moment?" Nana said and pulled Mama aside into her room. Julia trailed behind. "Stay here, Julia."

"No, I want to stay with Mama." Nana sighed, but she did not fight it. She closed the door behind them. Elise sat on the bed. Julia climbed onto her lap and pretended to play with her locket while she listened in. Nana towered over them. "Are you feeling okay?"

"What do you mean? I feel great."

"That's what I mean. Why all of a sudden..."

"I thought this is what you wanted."

"Of course, I want you to be happy, but I'm just concerned that you are acting strangely."

"Why would you think that, mom?"

"You gave that green kimono to Juanita, the one your father sent you when you graduated from college. I thought you loved that kimono."

"I do. I just don't wear it and I thought it would look good on her. Is that what this is about? A kimono? I can get it back if it's bothering you so much."

"No, of course not. You can do whatever you want. It's your kimono. I just want to make sure that this isn't some kind of crazy episode..."

"Mother, I'm fine. Let's just leave it at that and enjoy the day."

"You do realize that there is a big hole growing in your yard?"

"Don't worry about the hole. Everything is going to be okay." Mama hugged Julia into her chest. Julia giggled.

"What do you mean?"

"Nothing. Just don't worry." Mama got up and grazed past Nana to open the door and left. Julia followed, calling after her. Nana crossed her arms over her chest, uncertain of the truth.

Julia noticed that the light outside faded from yellow to indigo. Nana and Mama walked into the kitchen to put together a plate of crackers and cheese. Julia watched them. She saw for the first time how they resembled each other, the way in which they gestured gracefully up in the air with their hands while speaking and nodded intently while listening. Nana stood a couple of inches taller than Mama, but Julia could see beneath the gray and wrinkles that they looked a lot alike. She hoped that she would also look like them when she grew up. She wasn't able to hear what they were talking about, but before they returned to the living room, they hugged, a big long hug that seemed to encompass a vast sum of love and distance.

Mama knelt down in front of Julia and held her shoulders firmly in her hands. Mama gave her that serious look, searching Julia's eyes for understanding. Julia thought she was in trouble, but then Mama said, "I love you, Pumpkin. Don't be afraid." She stood up and looked around the room.

"Well, folks," Mama exclaimed as Nana set the plate of food on the coffee table. "Thank you so much for being here. It means so much to me. Goodbye."

Everyone looked at her perplexed. Mama grabbed her dress up above her knees and sprinted out the open door. People jumped up from the chairs, sofas and floor to follow her outside. Julia saw Mama's muscular legs like a swift blur, felt the wind of her movement blow through her. For a moment, she knew the bliss of Mama's running, the freedom of moving fast, but then, her breath stopped inside her throat and her heart suspended in her little chest. Mama seemed to wave and smile as she lifted her arms up into the air and leaped boldly into the hole.

# Chapter Twelve

AFTERMATH

Inside the dark closet, surrounded by the soothing scents of Mama—fresh grass and curry, lavender laundry and wood smoke—Julia curled into a ball on the floor, pulling out shoes from beneath her and shut her heavy lids. She focused on the steady thud of raindrops on the roof like a somber symphony.

After Mama jumped into the hungry hole, there was nothing anyone could do but cry—the Circus Family, Juanita, Mr. Bob and Abe. Only Nana and Julia stood by calmly staring at the hole like something might happen. They slept in the yard the first few nights with the Circus Family and Farley and each morning when they awoke, the rim of the hole receded farther away. They were at once relieved and saddened.

Julia did not speak for three days while she followed Nana around. On the fourth day, when Nana broke down in tears while washing the dishes, Julia just watched her with remote fascination. When Nana quieted her sobbing, Julia finally spoke, "Why is the hole shrinking now?"

Nana turned to face her, "I don't know, Jujubean. I wish I could help you understand, but none of it makes any sense."

"Where is Mama?"

"I don't know."

"Is she coming back?"

Nana put down the dish she was drying and knelt down beside Julia. She clasped her hands and looked into her eyes with an expression that Julia knew to mean she better listen.

"I don't know where Mama is, Jujubean, but I can say for sure that she's not coming back. She's gone."

The question that troubled Julia then was, Why? Why did Mama do it? Nana couldn't explain. She just went about her business not thinking about it while Julia watched her—tidying up, mopping the floor, dusting the shelves. Why did Mama do it? Why did she leave Julia standing there, not sure whether to be sad or amazed? Mama told her not to be afraid, so she was going to make sure she got her wish. Julia was going to be the bravest little girl in the world.

So, when the monster appeared from the dark crevice of the closet, she was not afraid. A fuzzy shadow that lurched forward in short steps, it roared with horrible unrest. It did not want to share the closet with anyone and it was doing its worst to convince Julia to leave. It reached up and clawed the air while showing its terrible teeth. But Julia just roared louder until it cowered back into its hollow.

Nana called for her from the other room. The light from under the door had illuminated the closet just enough but suddenly it felt very dark. She pulled her knees up under her chin, waiting in the dark to be found. She rubbed at the locket around her neck.

Nana's voice trailed off into the guest room but she heard the thud of other feet against the tiles enter the doorway of the bedroom. They paused before the bed, pivoted and turned toward the closet. Julia held her breath and scrunched her eyes closed as if being unable to see would make her unseen. The door opened slowly and let in the daylight from the open window across the room. Julia looked up.

A man that she had never seen before stood at the closet door. He was tall with wheat-colored hair pushed off his face and small glasses in wire frames. He stared straight ahead into Mama's clothes, quiet as if witness to something sacred. He reached out and ran his fingers over the clothes, the skirts and blouses, sweaters and dresses. Then he gathered them up in his palms and buried his face in the fabrics, running his cheek over them and breathing deeply.

Julia had been trying so hard to be quiet that a defiant sound escaped from her throat. She brought her hand to her mouth to mute it, but it was too late. The man looked down at her. He squinted into the darkness of her hidden nook.

"Julia?" he said.

Julia stared at him suspiciously. She had never seen him before. He knelt down and she pulled her knees in tighter.

"Julia, what are you doing in here? We've been looking for you. Come on out. It's okay."

Julia did not move. She heard Nana call again as she entered the room. "Did you find her?" she asked the strange man.

"Yeah, she's hiding in the closet."

Nana came over to look. "Jujubean, what are you doing in there? I was worried. Come out and meet your..." Nana hesitated and looked at the man, "...your daddy." Julia's stomach filled with yellow butterflies. This was Daddy. He looked at her and smiled. She hid her face in her knees. "Well, I'll leave you two to get acquainted," Nana said and left the room.

"Thanks, Barbara," he said after her.

Daddy made himself more comfortable on the floor, rocking his hips into a final resting place. "You probably don't remember me, do you Julia? I haven't seen you since you were a baby and I'm sorry for that." All the times Julia daydreamed about meeting Daddy, she never expected an apology. She looked up. "You look so much like her," he said. Daddy's eyes began to glisten behind his glasses. He took them off and wiped them with his shirtsleeve. He had on a brown blazer and jeans. He seemed comfortable sitting on the floor of the closet beside her. Julia watched him, but did not speak.

"I loved Elise, your mommy, so much. I missed you both so much," he said, "I just wanted us all to be together." Daddy's eyes were pooling and he did not bother putting his glasses back on. He lowered his head and Julia watched his shoulders rise and fall with his stifled breath. After a while, he sat up straight, wiping his eyes again. He put on his glasses and looked right at her as if for the first time. "Hey, I recognize that necklace." Daddy reached out toward Julia's neck but she leaned away. He pulled back. "That was my grandmother's."

"I know," Julia said.

"Well, we'll have plenty of time to catch up. Let's go get something to eat." He slapped his thighs and pushed up to standing. With her hand secured in his long palm, she stood up.

They walked down the hall into the kitchen. Nana

had covered the hall mirror and all other mirrors with a sheet and said that they must stay that way for seven days. Julia did not ask why, somehow it made sense to her. Julia held tight to Daddy's hand for a long while, even as it began to get sweaty.

Outside the door, Farley barked and jumped to get the attention of someone that might let him in. He was drenched from the rain. Julia tugged at Daddy's arm. He looked down at her. She pointed outside.

"You want to go out?" Daddy asked.

She nodded.

"Okay, but don't go too far in case I want to find you again."

Julia smiled and let go of Daddy's hand. For a second, she had the sensation of falling away and had to catch her footing. "Are you okay?" Daddy asked. She nodded and ran for the door to see Farley.

She heard Mr. Bob's voice behind her ask, "How's she doing?"

Julia pet Farley under his neck where his fur remained dry. Farley began to walk toward the field. Julia followed.

Farley veered to the right of the field, making a wide arching path around the area where the hole and tree had once been. Though the physical manifestation of the hole vanished, the void it left behind remained. Neither Farley nor Julia dared trespass in that field. They circumnavigated the rim as if the hole was still there.

Julia followed Farley across the river and continued to follow him as he made his way up a narrow path of switchbacks along the canyon wall. Farley stopped every so often to look back and check if she still followed. Julia leaned down and held a rock to help her balance. Her dress was already muddy below the waist. The path kept climbing through the junipers. She slipped a little on some gravel but stood back up. She stopped and turned around.

Down below, she could see their little house and the Gallegos Ranch where the green circus bus was parked along the river bank. She felt the chill of the breeze on her bare arms and wondered how much longer the Circus Family would stick around. She wondered what else might change.

Just before she and Farley reached the rim of the canyon wall, Farley cut east toward the mountain. Julia had never been up this high, had never seen the mountain from this perspective. She felt as if she could reach out and touch it. Instead, she held her hands out in front of her like a bowl for the distant peak to perch upon. She squinted and stared at the way depth can disappear, the world could flatten and lay still for her. She waved at the mountain. This much closer, it must be able to see her. She waved again, hopefully. Farley whimpered impatiently.

Thunder echoed in the distance. She looked up at the sky and wondered if it would rain again. Julia felt her stomach tighten with longing for Mama, her stories, the feel of her hair, the smell of her skin, her arms holding her.

She decided to climb higher to the ridge top. Farley followed her close behind. She wanted to see the construction site. It had been a long while since Nana and Mr. Bob took her to the development.

The last part of the climb was the steepest as she scrambled up the hillside. When she finally reached the ridge top, she crossed an overgrown trail and climbed over some rocks to get a view.

Sweeping across the small valley below laid a patchwork of hard gray slabs and various piles of debris. Without the equipment and building frames, it looked like a wasteland. Along the outskirts, the forest already began to encroach. Julia got that feeling again. Her stomach tightening and her chest sinking.

"What do you think of all this Fa'ley?"

She didn't expect an answer, of course, but he looked at her in a way that let her know he understood. "You miss her too." Julia stroked his fur and he leaned into her. She was so used to him trying to get away from her that she was surprised by his new endearment. "I love you, Fa'ley."

When Julia returned to the house, Daddy sat at the kitchen table with Mr. Bob. Nana made tea on the the stove.

"There she is!" Nana exclaimed, "Where have you been?"

"With Fa'ley," Julia answered.

"Come sit, Jujubean. Let's talk."

Julia had been avoiding talking, avoiding this talk. She knew that the full extent of change was just beginning.

Daddy looked at her through his lenses, his eyes smiling with subtle awe. Nana told her that this was her daddy, so she knew it was true and everything else about him—his smile, manners, eyes—also told her that this was him. She remembered one of the last things Mama promised to her, "You will see him soon." She was right.

Nana served tea to Daddy and Mr. Bob and sat with them at the table. Daddy spoke, "Julia, I want you to come live with me. Would you like that?" He reached his hand out to her awkwardly and then withdrew it again. "I've waited so long to be with you. I wish it didn't have to be under these circumstances..." Daddy's mouth tightened and his eyes began to well up. Julia wondered if Daddy always cried this much.

Nana spoke, "Your daddy lives near a big city in another state, but not too far from here and he has a house there where you lived when you were a tiny baby." Julia had forgotten that she once lived somewhere else. "There are lots of kids there, too." Julia was excited about this, but she didn't show it.

"And you'll have your very own room," Daddy said.

"With flowers?"

"If you'd like."

Again, Julia was pleased but did not smile. She looked down at Farley. "What about Fa'ley?"

"Of course, he can come too." Farley wagged his tail.

"What about Nana?"

"Oh, Jujubean," Nana said, "I will see you all the time, but I have my own house, not far from where Daddy lives. It's been sitting abandoned for so long now. I hope the mice haven't taken over." She laughed oddly.

Julia was sad then. She wanted to be with Nana. Nana must have noticed because she said, "I'll come every weekend, at least for a while, how's that?"

"That's okay, I guess."

Still, Julia thought it was weird. Daddy was still a stranger to her. As familiar and nice as he seemed, she did not know him. He must have understood this because they decided to stick around until after Julia's birthday the following week to pack things up and say goodbye.

Daddy spent many quiet hours in Mama's room, putting things into boxes and not saying much. The first snow had already dusted the ground and melted away. One day, Daddy took Julia for a walk into the forest and she stopped him when they reached the special meadow. She did not tell him it was special. But then, he suggested that they walk farther. Mama had never walked with Julia that far into the forest. When, they came to an aspen grove, Daddy looked up and smiled. "Ah, here it is," he said. The leaves were golden and bright against the white bark and clear blue sky. The air felt cool and fresh with the scent of debris. Farley popped out of the trees every once in a while to check in.

"You know, I've been here before, with your mom, before you were born. In fact, she was pregnant with you, pretty far along if I recall."

"Really?"

"Oh yeah. You didn't know that? I'm surprised she never told you. Yeah, we climbed this mountain together, all the way to the top. We looked down at this little valley and the little speckled houses and imagined living here someday." Daddy looked over at Julia as she balanced on the ridge of a fallen tree. "Are you sad, Julia? About Mama? About what happened?"

"What happened?" Julia asked.

"I'm not sure," Daddy said. "I hope one day that will become more clear."

Julia thought about all the mysterious things Mama had taught her in her stories about fairies and witches, elves and monsters. "I know," Julia mumbled.

"What do you know, Julia?"

"Mama's in a magic world, far in the center of the earth where it is always night time, but the moon is always full. And there are dragons down there, nice ones, big blue-scaled dragons that breathe fire to light up the land. Mama is there now. She's playing with the dragons and with Tree."

"Is that so? Well, I hope you're right," Daddy said, "because that sounds wonderful."

Daddy looked down and smiled at Julia. She felt her chest tighten and she began to cry. He pulled her close to him and held her for a while. She cried even harder at his shoulder, but he never let go. He waited, quietly for her to pull back. Julia smiled up at him. "Feel better?" She nodded.

On the way back to the house, Daddy practiced some animal jokes on Julia. They weren't very funny, but she laughed anyway, sometimes so hard her eyes watered. Then, she taught Daddy some of her songs and he willingly accompanied her.

Julia turned five on Tuesday and that was the day they had her party. All the invitees were within walking distance and free of weekday constraints.

The Circus Family had already packed up and were waiting a couple of extra days in order to attend the party. They had plans to leave immediately afterward.

Before the party, Sunshine, Luna and Gypsy took Julia aside. They said they wanted some girl time with her before she parted for the big city. Julia felt like a big girl, sitting in the circle with the other women. Sunshine looked at Julia with her bright blue eyes, "We want to impart on you some very important information. Now, that your mama is gone..." her voice lowered when she mentioned this, "... and you are going to live with your Daddy, we wanted to make sure you knew about woman stuff."

"Woman stuff?" Julia asked.

"Well," Gypsy said, "It's knowing that girls can do anything boys can do."

"That girls should stick together and never compete for boy's attention," Sunshine said.

"I don't know any boys," Julia said.

"Well, you will," Gypsy said, "but it is important to remember to be yourself no matter what."

"Because you are beautiful just the way you are," Sunshine added.

"Yeah," Luna said, "Group hug." Julia followed as they spread their arms and moved closer together. She didn't understand everything they said, but she understood that she was part of something. She ran back to the house excited.

Nana was in the kitchen working on the birthday cake, chocolate with pink strawberry frosting. Julia looked in the yard for Daddy.

Throughout the day, Julia followed Daddy around, simultaneously clinging to him and observing him, asking often why he did this or that. He never grew tense or tired of her the way Mama used to. He hung balloons and streamers about the house, climbing a footstool to pin them to the ceiling. Julia watched from below.

"What are you doing?"

"Putting up party streamers."

"What's that?"

"Tacks."

"What do they do?"

"Hold up the streamers."

"Why?"

"Gravity. What comes up, must go down."

"Why?"

"Well, gravity is what keeps us on the ground and keeps the sun and moon in the sky. Look, if I let go of this tack what will happen?"

"I don't know."

"Will it float in the air?"

"No, silly, it will fall to the floor."

"That's right. And that's gravity."

"Can I help?"

"No, sweetie, this is too dangerous for you. Go see if Nana needs help."

Juanita arrived early while Nana was putting out snacks. She had a small bag with her that she immediately handed Julia. "*M'jita*," she said, "How old are you now? *Cinco*? Five? Such a big girl." Then her face turned sour. She turned to Daddy, "If only her mama was here." Daddy said nothing, only smiled down at Julia. She smiled back.

Soon, Mr. Bob arrived. He had a big box wrapped in yellow flower paper. He handed it to Julia. "For the birthday girl!" he bellowed. "Do you feel older?"

"I'm five."

"So big!"

"Did you say, 'Thank you,'" Nana asked entering the room.

"Thank you," Julia sang.

The adults gathered in the kitchen to drink coffee

and Julia shook her big box, listening to the small rattling sound inside, anxious to open it. No one had ever given her a present that big before and wrapped so neatly in patterned paper.

"Hello?"

She heard a lovely voice call through the screen door. It was Gypsy. Sunshine, Sparrow and Luna followed close behind. Sparrow hid something. "What do you have behind your back?" Julia asked.

Sparrow pulled out a doll, nearly as big as Julia, with yellow yarn for hair and blue buttons for eyes. Julia reached for it to take it in her arms, but the doll began to move. Its arm reached out to the side and its mouth opened wide to say, "Hello. My name is Flower. What's yours?"

"Julia."

"That's a beautiful name. I heard today is somebody's birthday. Whose birthday is it today?"

Julia pointed to her chest.

"Yours?! Well, then, I must belong to you."

Julia smiled as Sparrow passed Flower to her and showed her how to make the mouth open and close when she spoke and how to move her arm with a small stick. "For the birthday girl!" he said, "From all of us."

Julia looked Flower over and wondered why she didn't have any legs. Later, she put on a puppet show for everyone, then opened her presents. Juanita gave her a dress. She liked it, but she was so excited for Mr. Bob's gift that she threw it aside quickly and tore open his wrapping paper. Inside was a big box and in the box was a clear plastic lining and attached by small wires behind the lining were three toys. A dump truck, a back hoe and a bulldozer. Julia, ecstatic, asked Mr. Bob to get them out of the box immediately, so she could play with them.

In a while, the lights dimmed and everyone sang Happy Birthday. Julia closed her eyes, wished for Mama and blew as hard as she could, dispersing bits of spit across the cake. For a second, she thought she felt her there and then there was smoke. The light came back on.

Later, they gathered outside to say goodbye to the Circus Family. Gypsy knelt down beside Julia and gave her a hug.

"Are you sad to leave?" Julia asked her.

"No, I'm ready. How about you? Are you sad to leave?"

"A little."

"Why?"

"I'm scared to go to a new place."

"Well, you'll be with your Daddy and Farley, and Nana will be close by."

"Mama told me once that we were far'in-ers and would always be far'in."

Gypsy leaned in close to Julia's face, her voice lowered, "Well, Julia, we all are foreign in some ways, but one thing I've learned on the road is that we belong to people, not places." Julia smiled big. "I'll miss you, little one," Gypsy said and gave her a hug before loading into the bus. Luna yelled out the window, "Bye!" and waved to Julia who yelled the same thing back. They stood in the driveway and waved goodbye to the green circus school bus bumping and thumping down the road and disappearing as if it was never there.

Before long, Julia's turn to leave arrived. Daddy packed the car full of Julia's toys and buckled her into the backseat next to Farley. Mr. Bob, Nana and Juanita gave her kisses and promised to see her soon. She watched them waving at her as they pulled out of the driveway. She took one last look back before the house disappeared out of sight, back at the empty field, autumn's dusk light gilding the dry waving grasses.

# Chapter Thirteen

### Ever Afterlife

Elise spied subtle white butterflies circling overhead. One landed on her nose and spoke, "Open your eyes, Elise." What a sweet voice, she thought, like a song. She tried to open her heavy lids, but the butterflies sat on her lashes, a blur of thick fur, their bodies brown and soft as cattail tips. "Open your eyes," they insisted. She trembled and butterflies scattered. She opened her eyes. A young girl hovered over her. "Let's play," she beckoned, "let's play."

Elise turned her head from side to side, the soft grass tickling her cheekbones. A bright silver light shined on the familiar meadow. "Come," the young girl urged, pulling at an invisible rope that seemed to work to lift Elise from the ground to standing on her unsteady feet. Face to face, the girl was her exact height and a mirror image. She reached her hand to her face and her hair to feel that she was still there.

Her eyes were still adjusting to the soft haze surrounding everything. Elise was unsure, but she thought she saw twigs protruding from the girl's blonde curls. She was dressed in head to toe pink including a taffeta tutu and her clothes were two sizes too small. Her pants barely met with her ankle bones and the bottom of her shirt did not quite meet the waist of her tights.

Elise looked down at her own clothes, her favorite purple dress.

"What's your name?" she asked the girl.

"Julia, silly," she said, "Come on, let's go."

Elise wondered if she had school in the morning, if her mother was worried, how she ended up in this forest at night, but Julia just smiled at her like nothing else mattered and so, Elise followed her through the meadow and into the aspen grove. A dog joined them, but Elise did not recognize it. They ignored it until it disappeared behind some trees.

"The dragon is coming," Julia said.

"Not really," Elise smirked.

"Of course not, but let's pretend."

"Okay."

And they screeched at the invisible dragon as they ran laughing deeper into the woods. Julia stopped in her tracks, "Look, a caterpillar, one of those big fuzzy ones."

Elise stopped too and they knelt down to get a closer look. Julia picked it up and put it in her palm. She flicked her fingers at it, but it didn't move.

"I think it's dead," Elise said.

They both stared. The full moon disappeared behind a cloud. And they stood up, squinting at the caterpillar as if it might awaken at any moment.

"My friend died," the words gushed from Elise's mouth like a dam broke open and she felt silly.

"I'm sorry," Julia said. A soft breeze blew around them and Elise felt a chill. "My mother died," Julia said.

"I'm sorry."

Julia put down the caterpillar and they continued their walk, but Elise could not shake her sadness. "It's okay," Julia comforted her and Elise nodded.

Julia gasped loudly and Elise looked up to seek the cause. "The dragon!" she yelled and began to run. Elise laughed and ran after her. They ran and ran, white butterflies following close behind.

Photo by Judith DeBiase

JOHANNA DEBIASE writes from New Mexico where she is spellbound by the energy vortex of Taos Mountain. Originally from New York, she earned her BA in Literature and Creative Writing from Bard College and her MFA in Creative Writing from Goddard College. Her short fiction has been published online and in print including *Portland Review*, *theNewerYork*, *Monkeybicycle*, *Convergence*, *Prick of the Spindle* and *San Antonio Current*. She has also received scholarships to attend the San Miguel Writer's Conference, Vermont Studio Center and Rensing Center. The rest of the time, she is a certified yoga instructor, vintage clothing boutique owner and mother of one.

Other Books in the Wordcraft Series
of Fabulist Novellas

Double Monster Features by Peter Grandbois

*#1: Wait Your Turn/The Stability of Large Systems*
*#2: The Glob Who Girdled Granville/The Secret Lives of Actors*
*#3: The Girl on the Swing/At Night in Crumbling Voices*

For other titles available from Wordcraft of Oregon, LLC
please visit our website at:
http://www.wordcraftoforegon.com

Also available through Ingram's, Amazon.com,
barnesandnoble.com and by special order
through your local bookstore.

CPSIA information can be obtained
at www.ICGtesting.com
Printed in the USA
FSOW01n1514240215
5330FS